BATHING BEAUTIES, KNOBBLY KNEES AND MUSIC BY THE SEA

Bathing Beauties, Knobbly Knees and Music by the Sea

The Marina, Great Yarmouth
1937 - 1979

POPPYLAND
PUBLISHING

Colin Miller

First published 2019 by

Poppyland Publishing, Lowestoft, NR32 3BB

www.poppyland.co.uk

ISBN 978 1 909796 58 4

Designed and typeset in 12 on 14.4 pt Adobe Caslon Pro

Contents

Foreword

If you take a stroll along Great Yarmouth's vaunted Golden Mile, between the Britannia and Wellington Piers, pause occasionally to look above the hotchpotch of predominantly ground-level enterprises like amusement arcades, cafes and snack bars, ice-cream vendors and fast-food outlets. It might well surprise a stranger to our seafront that an upward glance will reveal that there is, or was, some elegant architecture to be seen, dating back to the 19th century but probably unappreciated by the holidaymakers and day trippers enjoying all the sights, sounds and smells of the highly commercialised Marine Parade.

However, Yarmouth's so-called Golden Mile and the attractions on the unsurpassed central beach were showing their age between the 1918 Armistice and the mid-Thirties. The entertainment provision was in a time-warp, the amenities still catering largely for visitors wearing "Sunday best" - the conventional street clothing they donned for high days and holidays regardless of hot summery weather at the seaside. Great Yarmouth, the East Coast's premier holiday resort, needed to be catapulted into the new more laid-back and relaxed age of the 1930s. It was an opportunity to be inventive and far-thinking, to achieve that worthy goal but without burdening the borough's ratepayers with a long-term strain on their pockets - in other words, it required maximum income from the visitors. But how was this to be achieved? What would chime with 1930s visitors?

It took many a meeting of the borough councillors charged with furthering the holiday industry, and members and officers endured furrowed brows as they sought a satisfactory solution. Eventually the council settled on an ambitious and inventive scheme well-nigh

The Marina, 1938

guaranteed to provoke opposition from many ratepayers - an open-air amphitheatre! Apart from the fact that the idea was bold and unconventional for a traditional British resort, most of the critics argued that such a building might be more suitable in sunnier climes. Wet weather here would limit its use and deter patrons from paying for admission if rain was forecast. It could become a wet elephant as well as a white one, figuratively speaking. There were also reservations that its continental style was out of kilter with its neighbours. But the progressives won the argument and the Marina was built, opening in 1937. It stood on a prime spot, was almost circular (officially, elliptical), with a stage/bandstand and seating for an astonishing 3000 patrons. What about the rain? Did anyone make provision for that likely event? Yes, the architects had allowed for that probability, providing room for sheltered seating around the perimeter walls for 1500 people, the same number as in the open-air accommodation.

For summers before and after the Second World War, the Marina buzzed with mainly low-brow entertainment, fun and games, bands, audience participation, beauty and knobbly-knee competitions. Audiences loved it, performers likewise, perhaps proved by the many seasons pre-and post-war that favourites Neville Bishop and his Wolves entertained there, mixing straight music with zany Billy Cotton Band Show type numbers. Neville Bishop's name became synonymous with the Marina. Some of the "bathing beauty" style competition finals were attended by nationally-loved show business stars appearing at our local theatres for the summer, invited to place the sash around winners' shoulders, their presence guaranteeing not only publicity but also that every auditorium seat was taken. However, times were a-changing for the UK holiday industry. British resorts, Yarmouth among them, became victims of the continental package holiday offering budget vacations by air and a near-guarantee of hot sunshine and cheap alcohol. So the dear old Marina, in hindsight perhaps designed more for the Costa del Sol than Yarmouth, was closed and demolished in 1979, one of its last uses being remodelled as Cow Town, staging Wild West shows. The site was redeveloped in 1981 as the current Marina Centre, its various leisure facilities including a lagoon-style indoor heated swimming pool with wavelets lapping on to its "beach" - now that building's long-term future is currently under official scrutiny.

Peggotty
nostalgia columnist
Great Yarmouth Mercury

Preface

Anyone holidaymaking in Great Yarmouth in the years immediately following World War Two will have fond memories of the Marina Theatre, an open-air music auditorium in a central position on the promenade that was described at its opening in 1937 as the most wonderful site on the east coast of England. The varying fortunes of the Marina during its forty-three year existence mirror closely the ups and downs of Great Yarmouth as a premier UK seaside holiday resort.

I was born on 5 August 1940 at Rollesby, a Broadland village eight miles from Great Yarmouth. During my summer holidays from school I often accompanied my mother on a midweek shopping trip into Great Yarmouth. The day usually ended with an afternoon at the cinema, but if the weather was fine we often went to the Marina. There we enjoyed an inexpensive afternoon's show of comedy, competitions and music from all genres; music that included excerpts from the classical repertoire, musical theatre and the popular songs of the day. Afternoon shows that not only entertained my mother and me but also had a defining influence on my knowledge and enjoyment of all kinds of music. I also remember the bands: the elegant Ronnie Mills and Harry Hudson at the piano, but the most popular of all was the infectious character Neville Bishop with his band, the Wolves. Alas, the theatre has long gone, replaced in 1981 by a leisure centre, a victim of the changing tastes in holiday entertainments. But for me, my recollections of the Marina bring back fond memories of the Great Yarmouth of my youth, especially of the 1950s when it was a vibrant and popular seaside destination and the undoubted flagship of the east coast holiday industry.

In this book I aim to trace in detail the rise and fall of the Marina theatre, the rationale and politics behind its creation and eventual demise, and the development of its unique and innovative style of entertainment, as well as providing details of the musicians, variety acts and entertainers who performed there during its lifetime. I will also explore other topics that were closely associated with the theatre such as its involvement in seaside bathing beauty competitions, post-war Battle of Britain celebrations, fund-raising carnivals and the attempted creation of a seaside municipal orchestra. I offer this book as a significant addition to the story of Great Yarmouth as a holiday destination and to the history of the British holiday industry in general, based on the inclusion of information and topics new to the public domain.

The information used to recreate my story of the Marina was derived almost exclusively from two primary sources; the editions of the many local newspapers held at the Great Yarmouth Public Library and the Norfolk and Norwich Millennium Library at The Forum in Norwich, including the Great Yarmouth Mercury, the Eastern Daily Press and the Eastern Evening News, together with the minute books of the Great Yarmouth Town Council and its numerous sub-committees that are preserved at the Norfolk Records Office in Norwich. Personal memories and other anecdotal evidence have been kept to a minimum. I have tried to be as accurate as I possibly can but inevitably there will be errors and omissions. Any conclusions and opinions expressed in the text are my own and are based on the evidence uncovered during my research.

As author I wish to acknowledge that this book would not have been produced without the help and advice that I received from many sources. Firstly, I must thank my wife, Dr Celia Miller, for her interest, encouragement and professional expertise, especially for her invaluable efforts in checking the accuracy of my manuscript and for correcting my numerous grammatical mistakes. I must thank Gareth Davies from Poppyland Publishing for his faith in the book and for his advice during the publishing process. My thanks also go to the staff at the Great Yarmouth Public Library, the Norfolk Records Office and the Norfolk Heritage Centre at the Millennium Library in Norwich for their help during the long days of my research. A special thank you is due to the Great Yarmouth Borough Council and its legal department for their efforts with identifying the provenance of many of the illustrations used in the book and for navigating me through the complex rules of copyright law.

An immense thank you is due to the well-known and much loved Archant newspaper columnist Peggotty for agreeing to write the Foreword for this book and for his valuable help and advice. My thanks go also to the individuals and organisations that have permitted me to source photographs and illustrations from their collections, including the Great Yarmouth Borough Council; the Great Yarmouth Mercury and the Photographic Archive of Archant Newspapers; the Norfolk County Council, Picture Norfolk and the Great Yarmouth Public Library. Where necessary, I have made every effort to identify, trace and acknowledge all the current copyright owners for their permission to reproduce these photographs and illustrations but in some cases this has proved an impossible task. I would be pleased to hear from any copyright holders regarding possible errors or omissions made in this book and I will make every effort to ensure that these are rectified in any reprint.

My thanks go to the following organisations and copyright holders for the illustrations identified in the text by number; Archant Newspapers Ltd (Archant) for 9, 11, 21, 24, 25, 33, 34, 37, 41, 43 and 48, Norfolk County Council and Picture Norfolk (NCC/PN) for 3 and 47, Great Yarmouth Public Library (NCC/YL) for 2 and 12, The Reepham Village Archive (RVA) for 6, and The Great Yarmouth Borough Council Planning Department (YPD/YL) for 44 and 45. Unattributed illustrations are from my personal collection of ephemera relating to Great Yarmouth and the Marina. This includes a small collection of memorabilia originally belonging to the musician Arnold Rack (AR) that he put together during the 1948 summer season while he was performing at the Marina with Neville Bishop and his Wolves. Among the illustrations I include a wide variety of advertising material produced on behalf of the Marina by the Great Yarmouth Town Council and other agencies and organisations. I have also indicated in the captions the original copyright holders (where they are known) of photographs, postcards and other ephemera that I believe are now considered to be in the public domain or where the current holders have been untraced.

Colin Miller 2019.

1

An Ambitious Plan

In 1935 the Great Yarmouth Town Council gave its backing to an ambitious scheme for improving the facilities offered to visitors and holidaymakers on the seafront between the Britannia and Wellington Piers in an attempt to consolidate Great Yarmouth's position as a prime holiday destination and to provide work for some of the many unemployed men in the borough. Based on an original suggestion by Councillor W.J. Larke, the proposal that was presented to the Beach and Promenade Committee by the Borough Engineer on 6 February 1935 involved the total demolition of all the temporary and permanent buildings and structures between the east side of the Central Marine Parade and the sea wall, including the existing open-air swimming pool, and for these to be replaced by a music bandstand, pavilion and enclosures, an underground car park to cater for the increasing number of motor vehicles visiting the resort, ornamental gardens, illuminated fountains and a badly needed public convenience. The development plan also included a proposal for the construction of a new up-to-date indoor swimming pool close to the Wellington Pier. The existing pool suffered greatly from the fact that it was not equipped with a filtration plant and consequently had to be emptied every week and re-filled again with fresh sea-water. The estimated cost of the scheme was put at £120,000; £80,000 for the redevelopment of the Central Parade and £40,000 for the construction of a new swimming pool. It was also suggested that the Central Parade development alone would provide badly needed work for over 200 unemployed men.

The proposal provoked a great deal of argument and debate among members of the Town Council regarding the type of facilities needed by Great Yarmouth in order to maintain its reputation for being a progressive holiday resort. Genuine concerns were expressed by some councillors regarding the exorbitant cost of the initial proposal and, as a consequence, the General Purposes Committee presented a modified scheme to the Town Council on 6 December 1935. Despite the call from many quarters for the construction of a multi-functional conference hall on the Central Parade, the new simplified scheme proposed only the building of an open-air bandstand and auditorium with some internal and external sheltered accommodation, formal gardens to the north of the auditorium, including a floral clock and ornamental fountains, and additional shelters along the promenade to protect visitors against the wind and rain often encountered during a British summertime. The swimming pool on the south side was to be retained but fitted with a new filtration plant. The estimated cost of the new proposal was a more acceptable £38,500. The underground car park proved to be an engineering impossibility due to the depth of the sand and the instability of the ground beneath the Central Parade. The scheme was duly approved and an application was immediately submitted to the Ministry of Health for a loan to cover the cost of the redevelopment. Following a request from the Recreation Grounds Committee, it was later agreed to replace the proposed formal gardens and floral clock by two Cumberland turf bowling greens, producing a further estimated saving of £580, although the loan requested by the council from the Ministry of Health remained at £38,500.

Work on the redevelopment began in early 1936 but was abandoned for the summer holiday season mainly due to the prevarication of the Ministry of Health in agreeing to the requested loan, which was not finally sanctioned until July of that year. Work began in earnest in the following September with the ambitious aim of completing the project in time for the start of the 1937 summer season. A special committee was established to oversee the project consisting of Councillor Morgan as Chairman, the incumbent Mayor (Councillor Perrett), Aldermen Brett, Goode, Greenacre, Harbord, Knights and Lawn together with Councillors Barr, Carr, Debbage, Gibbs, Grand, Larke and Weeler, the building works were placed under the supervision of the Borough Engineer, Mr S.P. Thompson.

When it was finally completed, the new development consisted of a large elliptical enclosed auditorium designed for musical entertainment with a sunken open-air seating area in the centre, stepped covered seating 24 feet in depth around the edge and a covered bandstand with dressing rooms on the eastern sea end; the whole large enough to cater for an audience of 1,500 in the open-air seating and a further 1,500 under cover. The roof of the covered area was made from reinforced concrete so that it would provide an upper terrace accessed by stairways from inside the auditorium for visitors to stand upon or sit on in deckchairs. The back of the covered accommodation was in the form of folding wood and glass screens which could be partly or fully opened to provide ventilation in hot weather. Opposite the bandstand, the main entrance and ticket office opened out onto Marine Parade flanked either side by large modern public lavatories for both men and women. As the east-west diameter of the new building was larger than the gap between the sea wall and the Marine Parade, it was necessary to modify the existing straight sea wall to accommodate and provide a continuous outer promenade around the enclosure. Two Cumberland turf bowling greens were laid to the north side of the auditorium but the south side remained undeveloped due to the retention of the swimming pool and was eventually used for car parking. Around the outside of the auditorium and along the seaside edge of the bowling greens, open-fronted shelters were provided with seating for use by the public. The roofs of the covered seating areas, both on the inside and the outside of the auditorium, were supported by colonnades of pillars giving the whole building a classical feel. All the walls and pillars were covered in cream terracotta tiles with a green and black design. A shield displaying the coat of arms of Great Yarmouth was located above the entrance and three illuminated fountains provided a decorative feature between the two bowling greens.

Because of the pillars, the General Purposes Committee recommended to the Town Council that the building should be known as 'The Colonnade', a suggestion that did not gain much support from the other members of the council. Various alternative names were suggested including 'The Casino' but, finally, a proposal by Councillors Bayfield and Gibbs that it should be called 'The Marina' was accepted, despite the council acknowledging the fact that an establishment of the same name already existed in Lowestoft. Once this was agreed, it was suggested that Marina, Duchess of Kent, should be invited to open the building, although this proposal was never followed through. Because of the prominent position of the public lavatories at the front of the building, many of Great Yarmouth's inhabitants henceforth affectionately referred to the building as 'The Latrina'.

As well as providing work for many unemployed labourers, the project gave a much needed economic boost to many national and local businesses. Among the many local concerns benefitting from work on the Marina were Dawnay's Ltd of Norwich who provided 100 tons of steel for the main structure of the building, R.H. Carter & Son Ltd of Southtown for all the woodwork and joinery, Cooper's Ltd of Great Yarmouth who supplied the sanitary fittings and 3,000 collapsible canvas armchairs for use as seating, Carr & Carr of Regent Street for supplying the microphones and amplification equipment, and Palmer's Department store for providing 200 deck chairs for hire outside the Marina and on the roof terrace. The council's own engineers were responsible for all the electrical work including the installation of the stage lighting and 3,200 neon tubes to provide a vivid red outline of the building after dark. When the Marina was finally completed, the Borough Engineer reported that rising prices had resulted in a final cost of £46,134, exceeding the original estimate of £38,500 by £7,634, and that an additional loan from the Ministry of Health would be needed to cover this excess. On completion, the control and management of the Marina was passed to the Beach and Promenade Committee, including all decisions regarding the form of entertainment to take place inside the auditorium and the recruitment of staff and performers, while control of the bowling greens was given to the Recreation Grounds Committee. The Marina finally opened for business on 1 July 1937 and the two bowling greens four weeks later on 29 July.

From a modern perspective, the decision to build an unroofed music auditorium in a prime position on the seafront for use only in the summer months seems an impracticable choice but at the time it was the logical conclusion for most of the Committee. Compared to many other towns Great Yarmouth was thriving, even in the depressed times of the 1930s.

> Next to Norwich, Yarmouth is the chief town of the eastern counties, and the port of East Norfolk and Suffolk; it is a flourishing town, owing to its fisheries, its foreign trade, its advantages as a popular seaside resort and bathing place, and its manufactures.[1]

The port, market, retail premises, fisheries and small factories provided all year-round employment for most of its inhabitants. While from June until September the holiday trade swelled the population not only with holidaymakers but also with the casual labour needed to staff the hotels, guesthouses, cafes, restaurants and entertainments along the seafront. Like many other English holiday resorts, Great Yarmouth gained some benefits from the depression of the 1930s as vacations abroad became more expensive and were considered to be unpatriotic.[2] As soon as the holiday season ended, the town was invaded once more; this time by the North Sea herring fishing fleet and the land-based workers needed to process the catch, mainly young Scottish fisherwomen. Outside their respective seasons, the facilities used by the holiday and herring fishing industries often lay empty as the rest of the town continued with its normal everyday working life. In the summer months Regent Road and the Marine Parade were filled with holidaymakers, but in the winter they were often deserted, the shops, cafes and amusements closed and their owners and workers gone, many returning to their homes in the Midlands. Therefore it was not surprising that the council was ready to accept that the Marina would be unused out-of-season. The projected income from its summer entertainments was considered sufficient to justify almost eight months of virtual inactivity.

Furthermore, from Victorian times a tradition of outside live musical entertainment on the beach during the summer season had become well established in most seaside resorts, including Great Yarmouth. In an era before radio broadcasting, local entrepreneurs as well as national sheet music publishing companies leased the best sites on the beach

1. A Valentine's postcard showing the Marine Parade in 1909. The popular Singers' Ring can be seen on the beach behind the public toilet block.

at most resorts from their respective town councils and hired troops of musicians to perform concerts in the open-air, promote new songs and sell sheet music, often behind fenced enclosures. In 1881, a local entrepreneur, 30 year old James Chappell Dorsett (often referred to as simply James Chappell), a self-styled Advertising Agent and Entertainments Manager from Great Yarmouth, leased a singing stand from the Town Council on the site that the Marina was to occupy 56 years later. The stand, known thereafter as Chappell's Singers' Ring, was a circular enclosure made of wood fencing topped with canvas that was equipped with a stage facing away from the sea, decorated with plants and lamps, and lit by gas. Customers paid a small fee at one of two small entrances to sit on benches and listen to the concert style musical entertainment taking place inside. 'Bottlers' collected contributions from holidaymakers outside the enclosure who were listening for free to the performances inside. These collectors were referred to as 'bottlers' because the contributions they collected were dropped into a glass bottle. Once placed inside it was almost impossible to retrieve any money without first breaking the bottle. In the winter, the ring was dismantled, stored in a council owned warehouse to be erected once again in the following spring, all at the council's expense.

2. Chappell's Singers' Ring. Were Lenton and Turner female entertainers? (NCC/YL)

The first artists hired by Chappell to perform at the Ring in 1891 were Lenton and Turner, two singers of comic songs, who were succeeded in turn by various troops of black-faced minstrels and gypsy violinists. When Chappell died in 1907, the lease passed to his daughter, Sarah Lawton, who continued Chappell's business for few more years. In 1915 the firm of Francis, Day & Hunter, sheet music publishers from London, took over the lease and employed various concert parties to promote their songs and sell sheet music, including well known touring troupes such as Frank Gee's Troubadours and the Jack and Jills. In 1932 Francis, Day & Hunter ceased promoting concert parties and withdrew from the lease, which then passed to a Mr Roy Cowl, a nationally known entertainments manager, who established a concert party at the ring performing under the name of The Yarmouth Queries.

FRANK GEE'S TROUBADOURS, GREAT YARMOUTH, 1927
Photo by Sarony, Great Yarmouth

3. *Originally formed from soldiers serving with the London based Kensington Battalion, Frank Gee's Troubadours were an all-male vocal ensemble. The Troubadours featured in concert parties at the Singers' Ring from 1907 until the early 1920s. This photograph was taken at the Sarony Photographic Studio on King Street in Great Yarmouth.*

4. *Frank Gee's Troubadours at the Singers' Ring. Sixpence for a seat on a deckchair was expensive in 1930. No wonder most of the seats are empty. (NCC/PN)*

By 1934, it was clear that the income from the Singers' Ring, being less than £100 in 1933, was uneconomical and that the site could be better used by the borough for other purposes because it occupied the best position on the promenade between the two piers. Consequently, the Beach and Promenade Committee resolved that after the 1934 summer season Chappell's Singers' Ring should no longer be used for concert parties. A sub-committee, consisting of Councillors Ellis, Johnson, Larke and Middleton and Aldermen Bayfield and Middleton, was formed to consider plans for the future improvement of the area. In November 1934 the Borough Engineer was instructed to draw up concrete proposals for the development of the site based on ideas put forward to him by the sub-committee. Conveniently, the Borough Engineer also condemned the Singers' Ring structure as being unsafe and a danger to the public, and so it was burnt at the end of the 1934 season and the seating given to the Wellington Pier. With this long tradition of a circular enclosure on the site for holding open-air concerts, concerts that had proved to be very popular with visiting holidaymakers, it was no surprise that the development plan that was presented to the council by the Borough Engineer in 1935 was basically an up-to-date modern brick-built version of the Ring – the Marina.

Although the Marina project appears in many ways now to be backward looking, its rationale was consistent with the accepted views of the time on the nature and purpose of a seaside vacation, as well as the Town Council's vision of the future for Great Yarmouth as a working town and holiday resort. Neither was it surprising for the planners to consider an entertainments facility open to the elements. The swimming pool was an open-air pool, roller skating at the Wellington Pier was on an open-air rink, the floral and water gardens were open to the air, the bowling greens, the pleasure beach, the promenade and the beach itself all encouraged the visitor to be out in the open-air. Despite a growing fashion for a healthy suntan, especially among the young, prior to World War Two most visitors to the seaside were there primarily to enjoy the salt water and the bracing and healthy sea air, and not in search of the sun. Older men frequently wore suits, jackets and hats on the beach while women dressed themselves in long-sleeved blouses and skirts and carried parasols to protect themselves from sunburn.

As well as tuberculosis (TB), which was endemic during the 1930s, a large proportion of the employees who spent their days working in the dusty and polluted atmospheres of many Midlands-based factories suffered from respiratory diseases and contemporary medical opinion recommended taking sea air to relieve these conditions. In the 1930s, the Town Council promoted Great Yarmouth as a centre for '*Happy Healthy Holidays*' with '*the most bracing air in England*'. At a conference of the British Health Resorts Association, held at Cromer in 1934, the delegates extolled the benefits of healthy air to factory workers and people suffering from respiratory disease, and stated that scientific evidence had indicated the east coast resorts of England were among the world's healthiest environments. Based on these long-held traditions and beliefs, the design of the Marina was a logical outcome and it was completely understandable that the redevelopment project should be financed by a loan from the Ministry of Health.

The opening ceremony that finally took place on Thursday 1 July 1937 was a most elaborate affair involving the best that Great Yarmouth could offer and designed to give as much publicity to the town as possible. Despite opposition from a few members of the Town Council, a sum of £200 had been allocated for the ceremony - a considerable amount of money at a time when the average weekly wage for British adult male workers was said to be £3..7s (£3.35)[3] and many national trade unions were unsuccessfully agitating for the adoption of a minimum wage for men of one shilling (5p) per hour. Among those invited to attend the official opening party by Mr Percy Ellis, Chairman of the Yarmouth Beach and Promenade Committee, were the newly elected Mayor & Mayoress of Great Yarmouth, Mr & Mrs H.T. Greenacre; The Lord Lieutenant of the County and High Steward of the Borough, Mr Russell Colman, accompanied by Mrs Colman; the Deputy Mayor of Great Yarmouth, Mrs A.M. Perrett; Arthur Harbord M.P. for Great Yarmouth; the Lord Mayors and Lady Mayoresses of Norwich, Ipswich, Southwold, Sudbury, Lynn, Lowestoft, Bury St Edmunds and Beccles; members of the Town Council and a special guest of honour, the popular Canadian-born star of stage and screen, Miss Victoria

Hopper. Her obituary in The Independent recorded that:

> The actress and singer Victoria Hopper, a petite blonde,
> was at the height of her popularity in the 1930s, when she
> starred in many films including *Lorna Doone* and *The Mill
> on the Floss*, appeared in the West End production of the
> Kern/Hammerstein musical *Three Sisters*, and was one of
> the pioneering performers on live television. Her marriage
> to Basil Dean, the producer-director who initiated the
> building of Ealing studios, gave a boost to her career,
> though inevitably there were accusations that he overrated
> her talents.[4]

The opening proceedings began at 1.00pm with a sherry reception
and lunch at the nearby Queens Hotel organised and hosted by the
hotel's proprietor, Mrs E.M. Nightingale. After toasts to the recently
crowned King George VI and to the Town Council and their invited
guests, the various Mayoresses and Miss Hopper were presented with
bouquets of roses by a diminutive but supremely confident two year old,
Annette Diamond. Each bouquet was created and supplied by Charles
Rowland & Company, florists of 153 King Street, from roses grown
by Messers Pitchers, market gardeners of Bradwell. All the ladies also
received a commemorative gift set of handkerchiefs that had been
manufactured at the Grout's Silk Factory in Great Yarmouth.

At 2.40pm the party processed the 100 yards along Marine Parade
from the Queens Hotel to the Marina, led by a cadet band of khaki-
clad buglers from the Yarmouth corps of the Norfolk Artillery. The
mayors and their attendants, who were all dressed in their formal regalia,
made a colourful spectacle for the watching crowds of townsfolk and
holidaymakers lining the route along the Promenade. At the Marina
they were led formally into the building by Mr Ellis, their arrival
announced by a fanfare from the buglers, and there they made their
way through the waiting audience to their designated positions in front
of the bandstand.

After the National Anthem was played by Art Gregory and his St
Louis Orchestra, the Marina's newly appointed resident band, Mr.

Ellis gave an introductory address to the 3,000 capacity audience in which he gave thanks to all those involved in the planning and construction of the Marina, describing it as one of the most wonderful sights on the east coast of England and expressing the hope that it would eventually develop as a conference centre as well as a venue for musical performances. After introducing the new manager, Mr Richard Courtney, to the public and presenting the Mayor of Great Yarmouth with a memento of the occasion – a small inscribed silver cigarette box with an engraving of the Marina on the lid – Mr Ellis called on the Mayor to formally declare the building open. The Mayor in turn expressed the hope that the Marina project demonstrated to the residents of Great Yarmouth the determination of the Town Council to develop the borough as the best and most up-to-date holiday resort on the east coast. After the building was formally declared open, there followed the first performance of the 1937 summer show *The Marina Melody Makers*, featuring Art Gregory's Orchestra, and during which the guest of honour, Victoria Hopper, sang a number of popular songs associated with her stage and screen appearances. The show ended with the first airing of *The Yarmouth March*, a musical piece specially composed for the occasion by the Marina's musical director, Frankland Winning, and arranged for Art Gregory's Orchestra by Walter Wild. Afterwards, the Mayor and his invited guests returned to the Queens Hotel for tea.

The two adjoining Cumberland turf bowling greens were opened four weeks later on Thursday 29 July by the Mayor. To celebrate the opening, the Norfolk County Bowls Association arranged a friendly match between the Norfolk men's bowls team and a representative side from the English Bowling Association. Thereafter, the Central Parade bowling greens were adopted as the location for the headquarters of the Great Yarmouth (E.B.A.) Bowls Club, as well as being available for hire by visitors and holidaymakers.

1   Kelly's Directory; Norfolk 1937.
2   Juliet Gardiner (2010) *The Thirties; An Intimate History*.
3   Miller J. "Note on the standard of living in Moscow in 1937", Soviet Studies 1953.
4   Victoria Hopper, Obituary, The Independent, 03 February, 2007.

CENTRAL PARADE & MARINA. GT. YARMOUTH.

5. An unattributed postcard of the Marina dated 1939. The warship patrolling near to the harbour's mouth is a clear indication that a declaration of war with Germany was imminent.

2

A Jewel in Great Yarmouth's Crown

The many fine words uttered at the opening ceremony by the Mayor and the chairman of the Beach and Promenade Committee failed to gain universal approval; not everyone was as enthusiastic about the Marina as they appeared to be. Concerns were raised in some quarters when it became clear that the council had placed all its hopes for the future on an uncovered and unheated bandstand where half the audience was open to the elements and its use was limited to the warmer summer months. Many suggestions were offered for ways in which the building could be profitably used in the winter, some reasonable, others unrealistic.

> May I suggest that it could be profitably converted to an ice-skating rink? The popularity of this winter sport can be judged by the gatherings on the Broads in suitable weather, but, as the conditions do not often suit the ice-skater, I think an artificial rink at the Marina would be greatly appreciated.[1]

The Great Yarmouth Hotels and Apartments Association had led the call for a covered conference hall on the seafront, not just because no such facility currently existed in the town but also because it would attract out-of-season visitors and much needed custom to their hotel businesses. Although it was the declared hope of the Town Council that the Marina should be used as a conference centre, it was already obvious to many that an open-air venue would not suffice. Others feared that the musical entertainment envisaged for the Marina was too similar to that already offered at the council owned Wellington Pier for both venues to be viable.

The early days of the Marina were not without their problems. The Town Council had decided that the Beach and Promenade Committee was to be responsible for the management of the Marina and, for that purpose, an additional budget of £2,000 was allocated to the committee's funds to cover the costs of hiring a general manager, temporary and permanent staff, and entertainers for the 10 weeks that remained of the 1937 summer season. It was also agreed that the revenue from all activities and entertainments held at the Marina should also be allocated to the Beach and Promenade Committee's funds. Yet, even while the Marina was under construction, the form that these entertainments should take was still undecided.

> In certain quarters the suggestion is put forward that an orchestra after the style of those that have been appearing in Sunday concerts in the town might be engaged. Coupled with this is another that individual turns might also be incorporated.[2]

As well as light orchestral and brass band music, the committee had also considered the possibility of commissioning plays, boxing shows and providing facilities for open-air conferences. Ultimately, the committee decided that the best course of action was to advertise for a modern dance band supplemented by individual acts. Applicants were invited to attend auditions in Birmingham and London during February and March 1937. Neither had the committee considered providing refreshments on the site, further indicating a possible lack of clear forward planning. Councillor S.H. Da'Volls was forced to complain that although the Marina was a wonderful building its potential was not being fully realised and that those visitors who were in need of refreshments had to go elsewhere.[3] As an interim measure, a kiosk was opened inside the building selling ice creams, lemonade and cigarettes. Catering facilities serving tea, coffee and light refreshments were finally installed in time for the 1939 summer season.

Another issue confronting the Beach and Promenade Committee was that of admission charges. As was the case for most seafront and park bandstands, the original notion was for free admission to the Marina but that a charge of 2d would be levied for the use of a chair. However, it soon became apparent that the budget of £200 per week barely covered the cost of hiring a first class band for the season and consequently it was agreed to impose a small charge for admission for the duration of the 1937 summer season - front stalls 1/-, stalls 9d, back stalls and lower terrace 6d, and top terrace 3d - despite some concern that charges would inhibit attendance. In addition, the Recreation Grounds Committee proposed making a charge of 6d per hour for hiring the Marina bowling greens, 2d for providing a set of bowls and 2d for shoes.

Employees' wages and Sunday opening proved to be further complicating issues. The depression had seen a lowering of the weekly wage for most workers and a reduction in the length of the working week, both affecting the weekly income of most households. These negative effects were offset slightly by an increase in the buying power of the pound. By the late 1930s, a government-sponsored house building programme and an expansion of the armaments industry enabled Britain to slowly recover from the worst of the depression. As this recovery strengthened, trades unions, labour councils and many sympathetic politicians were able to initiate improvements in working conditions for most employees, particularly blue-collar workers. The Factories Act of 1937 had limited the number of hours worked by women and children, and the average working week for men in employment had dropped to 48.5 hours[4]. As well as white-collar workers, by 1937 many blue-collar workers were also receiving a holiday of one week a year with pay, a right consolidated by the Holiday with Pay Act of 1938. Prior to this, time off from work was unpaid and for most employees trips to the seaside were financed through weekly savings put into a Holiday Club

fund. Employers, including many town councils, were also beginning
to accept the notion of a minimum working wage of one shilling an
hour, even if they were unable to implement it immediately. The Great
Yarmouth Town Council had insisted that any firm contracted to do
work for the corporation must be implementing a fair wage policy.

Therefore, it became a *cause célèbre* when it was clear that the basic
wage being offered on behalf of the Town Council by the Beach and
Promenade Committee to most of the employees at the Marina was
considerably less than one shilling an hour. Traditionally, because of the
type and seasonality of the employment and the nature of the employees
(mainly unqualified youths, itinerant workers, women and students),
many in the entertainment and holiday industries were poorly paid for
their services. A conference of the National Association of Theatrical
and Kine Employees held at the King Street Labour Club concluded
that, without the backing of a trade union, cinema attendants in Great
Yarmouth had become among some of the lowest paid workers in the
country, worse than workers in those distressed areas of South Wales
and the North of England that were still experiencing the effects of
high unemployment.[5] So, it came as no surprise that the wages being
offered to potential employees at the Marina were poor. In a letter
to the editor of the Yarmouth Mercury, Mr. W. J. Page reported that
cleaning staff and general attendants were being offered a basic wage of
25 shillings for a 72 hour week and cashiers 30 shillings.[6] Frank Stone,
Chairman of the Great Yarmouth Trades Council, cautioned that
industrial workers, with the benefit of union rates of pay, who were on
holiday in the town, might not support an entertainment facility where
workers were paid less than the nominal minimum wage for adult male
labour.[7] Although this immediate outcry did result in a slight increase
in the hourly rate offered by the Beach and Promenade Committee, in
1939 cleaners and attendants were still being paid a lowly 50 shillings
and senior attendants 52 shillings for a 60 hour working week. As
late as 1939, the council still declared itself unable to move towards
implementing a 40 hour working week and a minimum wage rate of
one shilling an hour for its lowest paid workers.

Attracting day visitors as well as holidaymakers to Great Yarmouth was a prime concern for the Town Council. Local day visitors usually arrived by car, bus or charabanc but those from further afield normally came on organised excursions by train. To ensure that such excursions were worthwhile, it was imperative that the town was able to provide more than just sand and sea air to entertain its guests, especially on Sundays. Like many seaside resorts, by the late 1920s Great Yarmouth had become lax in its strict observance of the outdated and draconian Sunday Observance Act of 1780. As a result, in 1932 the government introduced the Sunday Entertainments Bill which allowed limited Sunday activities where they had already become common practice or where local authorities and public opinion were in favour of their introduction. Cinemas were allowed to open on a Sunday but theatres were to remain closed; some limited musical entertainment was allowed but public dances and live variety shows were prohibited. By the late 1930s, the cinemas, the Marina, the pleasure gardens and bowling greens of Great Yarmouth opened on a Sunday but the Pleasure Beach remained shut. That Sunday programmes at the Marina were restricted to military band music and sombre musical concerts was a concern even for some members of the Town Council itself.

> Councillor W. J. Sayers asked by whose directions the Sunday programmes at the Marina were emasculated. Was it done to suit the various prejudices of certain people? Their duty was to consider those who were their customers and not what the committee thought they would enjoy. The Town Clerk said that the programmes were designed to conform with the provisions of the licence of the Marina.[8]

Not everybody was in favour of Sunday entertainments. The Sunday Entertainments Bill also included a clause that no worker should be expected to work seven days a week as a consequence of Sunday opening. However, it soon became clear that this clause was difficult to implement and during the summer season many employees were working seven days a week, willingly or otherwise. Some local residents and many religious groups were also strongly against any entertainments on a Sunday, although they appeared to be in a minority.

I see that the Council have decided to open the bowling greens all day on Sundays, thus providing the fears that Sunday play would be the thin end of the wedge to be all too true... The Council seems determined to ruin Yarmouth and drive away all decent visitors. If some heathen from darkest Africa were to walk along our front on a Sunday afternoon, what would there be to show him that this day is sacred to Christians? There is nowhere one can escape from this blatant heathenism. If one sits on the sea wall one is deafened from so-called music emitted from the Corporation owned Marina... And yet the Council refuse permission for the Open Air Mission to preach the Gospel on the foreshore. [9]

Despite these teething problems, the entertainment offered at the Marina was much appreciated by visiting holidaymakers. As a result of the interviews held in London and Manchester, the Beach and Promenade Committee had succeeded in putting together for 1937 the attractive musical variety show called the *Marina Melody Makers*. Richard Courtney from London, an experienced administrator in the entertainments business, was appointed as manager and Art Gregory and his St Louis Orchestra was installed as the resident band. The St Louis Orchestra was a well-known up-tempo dance band from London and its leader, saxophonist Art Gregory, was formerly musical director for the infamous Santos Casani, the man who danced the Charleston on the roof of a New York taxi, at his nightclub on Regent Street. Supporting Art Gregory were comedian Billy Matchett and singers June Calloway, contralto, and Mervyn Saunders, tenor. Throughout the season various well-known guest artists were engaged on a weekly basis including Victoria Hopper, the Four Aces, Jenny Howard and Ella Shields.

Known at various times as 'The Mirthquake' and 'King of the Old Time Music Hall', Billy Matchett was born in Toxteth, Liverpool and began his career as a comedian and raconteur at working men's clubs in the north-west of England.

He came to London in 1913 and his first appearance was at the Alexandra Palace, Stoke Newington. Later that year he appeared in his first of many pantomimes at the Opera House, Middlesbrough. Over the years he appeared in more than forty pantomimes, mostly as Dame.[10]

For most of his working life he featured as the resident comedian in summer variety shows at various seaside resorts, including Blackpool, Brighton, Margate and Southport as well as his 1937 visit to Great Yarmouth. A frequent broadcaster on radio and television, he often appeared on *Workers Playtime* and *Old Tyme Music Hall*, usually as the chairman. He returned to Norfolk in the early 1960s when he was master-of-ceremonies for the *Old Tyme Music Hall* at the Gorleston Pavilion Theatre.

Tenor, pianist and composer of popular songs, Mervyn Saunders was born in Bristol in 1910. A graduate of the Royal College of Music, he made his West End debut in Ivor Novello's musical *The Happy Hypocrite* before joining the cast of the *Marina Melody Makers* in Great Yarmouth. With a light tenor voice, he broadcast regularly for the BBC singing with many popular dance bands or accompanying himself on the piano in radio programmes that included *Melodies for the Late Evening*, *Grand Hotel* and *Dancing Through* with Geraldo and his Concert Orchestra. During World War Two he joined ENSA and entertained troops in Italy, Africa and the Far East. In 1947 he joined the cast of Big Bill Campbell's *Rocky Mountain Rhythm* singing as the character Sergeant O'Doherty. Performing with the BBC Revue Orchestra led to his own radio series which earned him the title of 'radio's voice of romance'.[11]

Born Daisey Evelyn Louise Blowers, Jenny Howard became a popular performer in musical theatre and was known as 'The Poor Man's Gracie Fields' due to her habit of recording covers of Gracie Fields' songs on the cheaper Woolworths label. Mostly she sung accompanied on the piano by her husband and manager, Percy King. In 1940, she moved to Australia where she had a long and successful stage career.[12]

Ella Shields was a popular music hall singer and male impersonator. She normally appeared on stage in top hat and tails as the character

Burlington Bertie. Best known for the songs *If You Knew Susie, Show me the Way to go Home* and her signature tune, *Burlington Bertie from Bow*, the latter written by her husband William Hargreaves and first performed by Ella at Newcastle in 1914.[13]

Not to be confused with the 1950s group of the same name, the Four Aces were an extremely talented English musical variety act referred to at times as 'The Human Orchestra' and 'Four Boys and a Guitar'. The basis of their act was to use their voices like musical instruments in an imitation of the more famous harmony group, the Mills Brothers, whom they tried to emulate.[14]

Under Richard Courtney's guidance, a weekly programme of events was established that became the format adopted during most of the Marina's subsequent years. Variety shows lasting approximately two hours were performed every weekday at 3.00pm and 7.30pm; and brass band and orchestral concerts at 3.00pm and 8.00pm on Sundays. As well as music from Art Gregory and his Orchestra and solo acts from the guest and resident performers, a different feature was added to the show each day including beauty contests, senior and junior talent competitions, comedy items and games for prizes. A special show for children was held every morning, organised and hosted by Billy Matchett, alias 'Uncle Billy'. If they wished, holidaymakers could visit the Marina to see a different show every day of the week.

The Marina's first season proved to be a great success. Selecting well-known top-class performers had attracted good audiences and by the end of September the income raised from all sources was just short of £6,600, a vast improvement on the £100 raised from the lease of the Singers' Ring. The new penny-in-the-slot lavatories alone raised nearly £700 and were clearly a much appreciated facility. At the end of the season, the Marina and its lavatories were closed and a caretaker was appointed to maintain and protect the property during the winter months, and to switch on the neon lighting and operate the fountains every Sunday evening.

For the 1938 summer season, the Beach and Promenade Committee had no hesitation in deciding to repeat the same style of entertainment that had been so successful during the previous year. And so a budget of £2,500 was allocated for engaging a 16 piece orchestra, a comedian and male and female solo vocalists for the summer season; Whit Sunday 4 June until Saturday 17 September. Following a series of interviews held in London by Councillors Glen and Harwood, Neville Bishop and his Orchestra were hired for a fee of £150 per week; an appointment that began a close and mutually beneficial association between Neville Bishop and Great Yarmouth which continued for the next twenty

6. *Following their success at the 1936 Crystal Palace National Brass Band Championships, the Reepham Temperance Band, conducted by Mr E.T. (Tommy) Ruffles, was often invited to play at venues in Great Yarmouth including the Marina. (RVA)*

years.[15] At the time, Neville Bishop and his Orchestra were under the control of the promoter Marius B. Winter and, as well as having just completed a successful tour of the Continent, were described as being one of Britain's leading broadcasting bands. In addition, the Norfolk based Reepham Town Brass Band, formerly the Reepham Temperance Band, was engaged to give performances of military music under its musical director E. T. (Tommy) Ruffles at the Marina on Easter Sunday and Monday for a fee of £35.

Neville Bishop and his 16 piece orchestra quickly established themselves as a class act at the Marina[16].

> Brilliant sunshine assured a promising season for the Marina when this year's resident orchestra, that of Neville Bishop, gave its first performance on Saturday afternoon. Many councillors and officials were present in the rather sparse company which gathered to witness the openings, but Yarmouth can congratulate itself on the very fine choice of entertainment provided. Neville Bishop is a conductor with an excellent discrimination. He possesses a great sense of humour that is definitely infectious, but his ability to put over entertaining numbers is his chief asset. His leadership makes the show go with a swing. He is adept on the drums and on a 'jazz set', chiefly composed of pots and pans, he presents a novel and amusing number.[17]

Performing in a style made popular by Billy Cotton and his Band, the orchestra not only played all kinds of music but also provided various comedy and solo musical acts from among their own personnel. The energy and enthusiasm of Neville Bishop as leader enabled him to quickly establish a rapport with all his audiences, young and old. Comedy was provided by Neville Bishop, George Hackford and Dick Spence (the latter often performing as Bishop's stooge); solo vocals were delivered by Ray Corston, tenor; Bill Davis appeared as a novelty one-man-band; tap dancing demonstrations were given by John Thomas; and Billy Kibel proved to be a competent impressionist. Solo musical acts were the province of Ronnie Thomas on harmonica, Billy Kibel on violin and N. Elston-Evans on cello. In George Hackford, Neville Bishop had acquired the services of an internationally renowned soloist, expert with two popular instruments of the day, the marimba xylophone and the vibraphone. Female vocalist Betty Belcher, soprano, featured in the Sunday concerts accompanied by Reg Mote on piano. Their success was such that the Orchestra was immediately re-engaged for the 1939 summer season.

> Attracting thousands of people each week, the Marina is proving the ideal holiday rendezvous. It provides excellent

NEVILLE BISHOP AND HIS FAMOUS BROADCASTING ORCHESTRA   PHOTO BY SARONY.
GT. YARMOUTH

7. *A publicity photograph of Neville Bishop's 1938 Broadcasting Band produced by Herbert Seaman's Sarony Photographic Studio at 28 King Street, Great Yarmouth. Seaman also owned photographic outlets at 23 Regent Road and 8 Marine Parade.*

8. *For the two summer seasons before the outbreak of war, Neville Bishop and his band regularly played to full houses. In this 1939 unattributed postcard, George Hackford's Marimba Xylophone is parked right of stage. The viewing platform known as the Revolving Tower can be seen in the distance. The tower was demolished in 1941.*

entertainment for all tastes and ages. Neville Bishop and his Broadcasting orchestra, apart from being a high class band, also presents a grand stage show in which the bandsman and their leader reveal themselves as most amusing entertainers. The eleven o'clock children's parties are a great success and at all the afternoon variety shows senior talent competitions are being held.[18]

In 1938, the BBC instigated a series of special live radio broadcasts from various important seaside resorts around the country. On Monday and Tuesday evenings, 12 and 13 July, the focus was on Great Yarmouth. The Monday evening featured excerpts from the summer shows at the Britannia and Wellington Piers while on the Tuesday a radio tour of the attractions along the Promenade ended with a concert by Neville Bishop and his Orchestra live from the Marina. In most of Great Yarmouth's shops, inns, hotels and guest houses, radios relayed the performance to attentive hordes of holidaymakers. The publicity gained from the broadcast was somewhat marred by the subsequent squabble among Town Councillors as to whether the 10 guineas (£10.50) paid by the BBC for Neville Bishop's services belonged to the borough or should be paid to the musicians. After an acrimonious debate in council, it was finally decided that each member of the orchestra should be awarded an appearance fee of 15 shillings (75p), at the same time acknowledging the considerable efforts that were being made by Neville Bishop and his band to establish the Marina as a major entertainment centre in the town.

By 1939, Neville Bishop and Richard Courtney had built on the foundations laid by Art Gregory to develop a style of entertainment at the Marina that was unique and ground-breaking, not just in Great Yarmouth but also compared with that offered in most other seaside holiday resorts. Had it not been for the outbreak of war in September 1939 and a discontinuity of five years in summertime entertainment, the Marina might have received a greater recognition for its contribution to the development of seaside entertainments than it subsequently has. From Monday to Saturday each week, shows began at 11.00am with *Uncle Neville's Children's Party*, followed at 3.00pm by a performance of

The Super Summer Show, a variety show of 'mirth, merriment and music' featuring music from Neville Bishop and his Orchestra and comedy and solo acts performed by individual members of the band. In the evening, from 7.30 until 11.00pm, the central area was cleared of seating for *Carnival Night,* a mixture of music, variety and dancing in the open-air. The innovative feature of all three shows was that the audience was encouraged not only to become actively involved in the entertainment but to provide part of the entertainment themselves; an idea originally devised and implemented by Richard Courtney, the Marina's manager.

The Marina's philosophy manifested itself in many ways. Audiences were encouraged to join in and sing when popular songs that they knew were being played and, occasionally, the band left the stage to parade around the auditorium followed by dancing adults and children alike, often exiting onto the Marine Parade and returning with additional followers in tow. Conga lines frequently weaved up and down the aisles, up the stairs and around the ornamental columns. Unsuspecting audience members were regularly coerced into taking part in comedy sketches, often to be gently humiliated but always leaving the stage with a smile. Competitions and games of one sort or another were a common feature of all the shows. Entertainments ranged from the more formal and prestigious bathing beauty, glamour and amateur talent contests to team games and more audacious contests such as the knobbly knees competition where men rolled up their trouser legs to have the 'knobbliness' of their knees judged by ladies selected from the audience. The bathing beauty and talent competitions were also regularly decided by the volume and length of the audience's applause rather than by a qualified panel of judges. Innovative new competitions were continually being introduced. In July 1938, the new weekly contest was a spelling bee competition for holidaymakers.

> Believed to be the first spelling bees ever organised for the public at large in a seaside resort, the idea represents an important step along the lines of organised entertainment for visitors. The competitive spirit has tremendous possibilities among holiday crowds, and the corporation is beginning to cash in on it. It has set a lead which other resorts will very probably be eager to follow.[19]

9. Members from the audience were encouraged to take part in competitions both serious and frivolous. The Knobbly Knee competition was always a favourite. (Archant)

Teams for the spelling bees were made up to represent different towns, hotels, camping sites, societies or clubs and competed in a knock-out competition. The first competition was won by a team from the Caister Holiday Camp.

In 1930s Britain, relaxing at the public house, visiting the cinema and going dancing were the main recreational activities for most ordinary men and women. Such was the enthusiasm for dancing it was estimated that up to 20,000 orchestras existed to cater for the need in the many dance halls, hotels and clubs throughout the country, making the decade a Golden Age for British dance bands.[20] In addition, smaller groups of local musicians played music for dancing in social clubs, village halls and the back function rooms of many public houses. Couples mainly danced waltzes, foxtrots, quicksteps and the veleta, while the music was subdued sufficiently for conversation to take place. Dancing provided a convenient opportunity for people to socialise and meet new friends. Many marriages were the result of a liaison on the floor of a dance hall. New dances were introduced on a regular basis; the Black Bottom, the Charleston, the Rumba and the Tango, but for the moment British tastes stopped short of adopting the energetic dances favoured in the USA; the Big Apple, the Lindy Hop, the Jitterbug and the Jive.

On warm summer evenings dancing in the open-air to the music of Neville Bishop and his Orchestra during *Carnival Night* at the Marina proved to be a popular attraction. Waltzes and quicksteps were interspersed with comedy from the band, competitions and instruction on new dances.

> In accordance with its reputation for being up-to-the-minute, the Marina will also present Park Parade contests. These will be staged by the Manager, Richard Courtney, and are expected to out vie even last summer's Lambeth Walk competitions.[21]

The Park Parade was a novelty sequence dance first introduced in George Black's production of *Black and Blue* at the London Hippodrome in 1936. The dances on the consecutive Fridays of 14, 21 and 28 July were further enlivened by the heats and final of the Hospital Carnival Bathing Beauty Queen competition. During the dark days in the run-up to the outbreak of World War Two, dancing at the Marina was a pleasant and energetic diversion.

> The largest attendance so far this season at the Marina was treated to a free lesson in the 'Boomps-a-daisy' on Saturday evening. This new dance craze caught on immediately and people on the promenade were provided with the spectacle of several hundreds of Marina patrons entering into the spirit of yet the oldest of the Lambeth Walk type dances around the upper deck.[22]

With the outbreak of war on 3 September the summer season was abandoned and the Marina, together with all the other holiday facilities in the town, closed its doors for the duration of the conflict. Even with a shortened holiday period, the Marina had admitted over 250,000 visitors to its various shows and had made a profit of £1,950. Over the next month, the audio equipment and neon lighting was dismantled and the grand piano removed into storage before the full-time members of staff were relocated to new duties and the Marina became incorporated into the coastal defence line established to counter the real threat of a German invasion.

1   Yarmouth Mercury, 28 August 1937.
2   *Ibid.,* 20 February 1937.
3   *Ibid.,* 28 August 1937.
4   Huberman & Minns (2007) *Explorations in Economic History* Vol 44, p538-567
5   *Ibid. 1,* 17 July 1937.
6   *Ibid.,* 7 July 1937.
7   *Ibid.,* 26 June 1937.
8   *Ibid.,* 8 June 1938.
9   *Ibid.,* correspondence 24 July 1937.
10   Billy Matchett 1889-1974 in www.the-music-hall.haisoft.net/laterv/LVBM.
11   Mervyn Saunders, Obituary by Denis Gifford in *The Independent,* 14 March 2000.
12   For details of Jenny Howard's life see www.itsahotun.com/thestars.
13   Roy Hudd,(1997) *Cavalcade of Variety Acts,* p168.
14   Information provided by Dave Ralph, musician.
15   NRO Y/TC 88/25 p236.
16   The musicians of Neville Bishop's 1938-39 Orchestra were Bandleader & drummer, Neville Bishop; Violins, Billy Kibel, Dick Spence, Eddie Hayes; Saxophones, Harry Smead, Stan Gibson, Russell Lenton, Bill Davis; Brass, Jock Melville, Jonnie Thomas, Peter Tompkins, Ray Corson; Rhythm, N. Elston-Evans, Howard Kershaw, George Hackford, Reg Mote, Ronnie Thomas.
17   *Ibid. 1,* 11 June 1938.
18   *Ibid.,* 5 August 1939.
19   *Ibid.,* 23 July 1938.
20   Juliet Gardiner (2010) *The Thirties; An Intimate History,* p624-7.
21   *Ibid. 1,* 27 May 1039.
22   *Ibid.,* July 1939.

3

Up and Running and in Good Shape

For the duration of the war, Great Yarmouth ceased to function as a seaside holiday resort. Its prominent position on the east coast of England, complete with a harbour and flat sandy beaches, not only made it an easy target for enemy bombers but also a potential landing point for invading forces. Consequently, the town quickly came under the control of the military and was heavily fortified, especially along the seafront. Various lines of defence were established in and around the town, with pillboxes at strategic points, tank traps and concrete road blocks. The beaches were mined and access to the promenade from the sea was protected by barbed wire, sandbags and other barricades. Many of the larger seaside properties were requisitioned for use by the defence forces, including the Marina. The middle section of the Britannia Pier was removed and explosives were laid to prevent its use as a landing stage for troops and supplies in the event of an invasion. Nearly half of the town's population of 50,000 civilians was evacuated to a safer location and many did not return until well after the war had ended.

Even after the threat of invasion had receded, Great Yarmouth suffered heavily from enemy bombing; 217 civilians were killed and over 1,800 properties were damaged or destroyed. But by 1945, with

MARINA BAND ENCLOSURE, GT. YARMOUTH

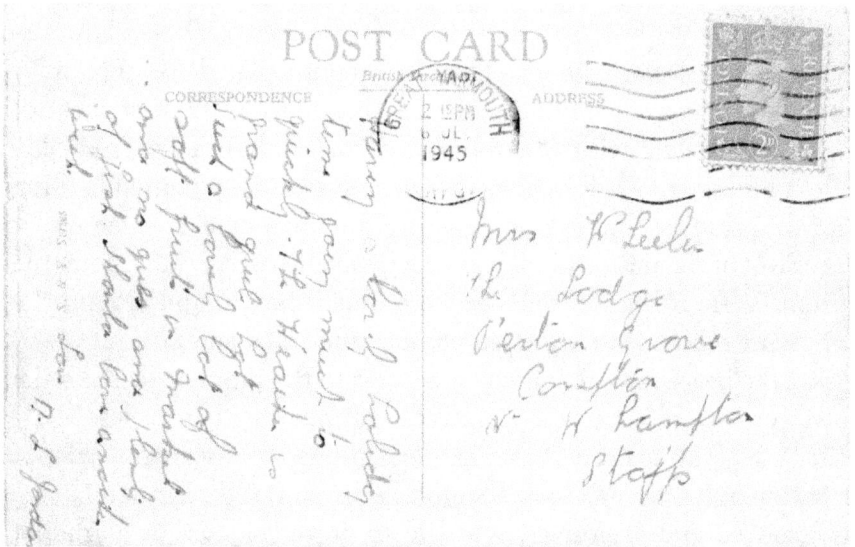

10. *A postcard from Great Yarmouth posted on 6 July 1945, a week before most of the town's facilities were up-and-running. Soft fruits, no queues and lots of fish were a bonus attraction, a welcome change from the shortages experienced in wartime Wolverhampton.*

the war in Europe nearing an end, the defensive obstacles were slowly being removed. The management of the Marina was returned to the Town Council and became the responsibility of the Entertainments Committee under the chairmanship of W.A. Thompson. On the assumption that hostilities were about to end, Mr. E.H. Gower was appointed manager of the Marina and preparations began in earnest for a 1945 summer season. Work was well under way to remove the barbed wire and barricades, and by January most of the concrete road blocks had been destroyed. The viability of a summer season depended greatly upon the ability of the Royal Engineers to clear a part of the beach for use by visiting holidaymakers. The Marina itself was made ready and all necessary repairs completed. On Sunday 7 May, two days before Germany's formal surrender, the Marina was back in use as the location for a service of thanksgiving organised by the Girls Training Corps to mark National Cadets Day, followed on 21 May by a victory service of thanksgiving and on 28 May by a concert performed by the Royal Norfolk Regimental Band in aid of War Charities Week.

As early as March 1945, the Entertainments Committee had made contingency plans for a limited summer season and interviews were conducted inviting artists to apply for employment as entertainers at the Wellington Pier, the Winter Gardens and the Marina. David Miller and his Broadcasting Orchestra were eventually booked to appear at the Marina for a ten week season commencing on 30 June. However, despite the war ending in May, the start of the Marina's summer season was unexpectedly delayed. Due to illness, David Miller was forced to withdraw his services and a replacement band was needed at short notice. Miller was eventually succeeded by Billy Bevan and his Band from Southport, who were engaged for the season at £225 a week, featuring singers Betty Taylor, Ted Bevan and Denis Calvert. The mine clearance that had begun in March on the section of beach between the Britannia Pier and the Jetty had also been slower than expected and a large section of the seafront and Promenade remained closed. This dangerous task was finally completed on 13 July when the whole of the Promenade was declared safe and a small section of the beach open for visitors. From 13 July, band concerts were held at the Marina every afternoon at 3.00pm and on Mondays, Wednesdays, Fridays and

Sundays at 7.30pm. On Tuesday, Thursday and Saturday evenings, the Marina was cleared of chairs for dancing in the open-air.

The importance of re-starting Great Yarmouth's holiday industry was not lost on Mr Thompson, the Entertainments Committee manager.

> If we had neglected what may be the first post-war season and provided absolutely no entertainment, then we would have found our business gone.[1]

The greatest problem he faced was the lack of available accommodation. Many of the hotels and boarding houses had been damaged or destroyed by bombing, and some landladies and hotel proprietors had yet to return. To kick-start the holiday season Louisa Rump, the Town Council's Publicity Committee manager, made an appeal to the remaining population of the town for help and compiled a list of those residents willing to provide bed and breakfast accommodation for prospective holidaymakers. Nevertheless, it was well understood that for 1945 at least most of the town's summer visitors would be day-trippers. The primary purpose for the Entertainments Committee in organising summer entertainments so soon after the end of the war was to advertise to future holidaymakers that Great Yarmouth's holiday industry was up-and-running and in good shape. It did not help that the visitors on August Bank Holiday Monday were drenched by a severe long-lasting thunder storm.

Great Yarmouth's Entertainments Committee was determined that the following summer of 1946, the first full post-war holiday season, should be a great success. Consequently, in an attempt to improve Great Yarmouth's standing as a first class holiday destination, one that would appeal to visitors from all levels in society, the newly elected Chairman, Councillor Moore, and other members of the Entertainments Committee made fact-finding visits to various seaside resorts to inspect their entertainment facilities and observe their preparations for the coming summer season. Among the many ideas that evolved from these visits was the suggestion that Great Yarmouth would benefit from the creation of a Municipal Orchestra along the lines of those orchestras that had proved extremely successful in other seaside towns, particularly

Bournemouth, Brighton, Hastings, Whitby and Scarborough.

In proposing the formation of a Municipal Orchestra at a spring meeting of the Entertainments Committee, Councillor Moore suggested that it should not be a symphony orchestra playing only classical pieces but one similar to the Harry Davidson Orchestra that played music for Old Time Dancing on the BBC radio programme *Those were the Days*. Not everyone was in favour of the idea. Councillor Barron suggested that its musical offering would appeal to only a few and not to the majority of the town's working class visitors. If the choice was between *"Champagne and oysters or chips and tripe"* he said, then most of Great Yarmouth's holidaymakers would prefer the latter.[2]

Also high among their deliberations was how best to use the Marina as part of the Council's own contribution to the summer holiday entertainments in the town. Initially, the committee proposed to engage a dance band, supplemented by guest artists, to provide a variety show at the Marina in the style that had become so popular before the outbreak of war. However, some councillors objected to this suggestion, arguing that this simply duplicated a form of entertainment already adequately provided for elsewhere, including at the council-owned Wellington Pier complex. Once the idea of a Municipal Orchestra had been mooted, many committee members not only approved of the idea but also immediately considered that the Marina, a modern up-to-date bandstand, was the natural choice of venue for its performances. While there was a majority backing for the idea of a Municipal Orchestra, others considered that the Marina, with its prime position between the two main piers, was not an appropriate location for such an old style orchestra. Alderman Stone said that the committee should adhere to the original suggestion of a dance band with guest stars because a Municipal Orchestra would not have the same potential to attract visitors and make as much money.

Despite further resistance from a few members of the Town Council, it was finally decided that Mr George Francis should be engaged by the Entertainments Committee to form a Municipal Orchestra consisting of a musical director and 26 musicians, which would be based at the Marina for the 1946 season from 30 June until 7 September at a cost of £320 weekly. George Francis was a conductor of national standing who had worked with many of the country's foremost orchestras. He studied music under Theodore Edward Aylward jnr., principal organist at Llandaff Cathedral. During World War Two he understood fully the morale boosting effect of music and strove to make music available to everyone, for which he was awarded the War Office special certificate for musical theory and instrumentation. Among his many accomplishments in 1942 he was appointed as deputy music director to Walford Hyden in the revival of *Lilac Time* at the Stoll Theatre in Kingsway, London. He also conducted the music to Verdi's opera, *Macbeth*, and the ballets *Les Sylphides* and *Fête Bohème* at the Lyric Theatre. In 1943, he became orchestral manager of the National Symphony Orchestra and on various occasions both conducted and played with the BBC Symphony, the London Symphony and Philharmonic, and the National Symphony Orchestras.[3]

At their April meeting, the Entertainments Committee agreed a summer season programme for the Marina that consisted of weekday gramophone concerts and Sunday military style band concerts for the period between 1 June and 29 June. For the remainder of the summer, daily music was to be provided by the newly formed Municipal Orchestra with special guest solo artists every Sunday. A special programme of music was also agreed for the Whitsun Bank Holiday weekend, 8, 9 and 10 June, which had been designated as Victory Weekend, a national holiday to celebrate the first anniversary of the ending of the war. The popular Norfolk-based Reepham Town Brass Band, under its musical director Mr E.T. Ruffles, was once again engaged to provide the early season Sunday and Victory Weekend concerts at a cost of 15 guineas (£15.75) a day. The guest artists invited to appear with the Municipal Orchestra at their Sunday performances included Marion Lowe, a soprano from the Sadler's Wells Operatic Company; Herbert Tree, tenor; Olwen Price, contralto; William Booth, tenor; Marie Stuart, soprano; Ronald Gibbs, baritone; Patricia Davies, soprano; and two end-of-season appearances by Peggy Taylor, soprano, on the 6 and 7 September. In addition, the Town Council received an invitation from the BBC for the Municipal Orchestra to perform in a number of special live concerts to be broadcast from Great Yarmouth during July and August.

The Municipal Orchestra's debut performance at the Marina was held on Saturday 31 June in brilliant sunshine. In their opening speeches, Councillor Moore and Mr J. W. Beckett, the Mayor, both welcomed the move away from dance bands at the Marina and expressed their confidence that the new arrangements would prove to be a great success. Councillor Moore stressed that:

> No longer can the reproach be levelled that only one section of the public taste is catered for in our municipal entertainments… The council had asked for something fresh and this would be the first time something fresh had been tried at the Marina.

In support of Councillor Moore, the Mayor stated that:

> At present our musical life is too often unnaturally divided between classics and jazz, with a much-to-be-regretted neglect of a whole school of music, whose gaiety, finesse and essential civilisation have never been equalled. In its concerts, the Municipal Orchestra, under its director, Mr George Francis, will play the type of light music which is pleasant to the ear and which will reward attention, at the same time providing relaxation for those who do not care to attend too closely.[4]

It soon became clear that the Municipal Orchestra at the Marina was not attracting large audiences and the attempt to educate the public to listen to and appreciate traditional and classical styles of music was failing. While *Showtime* at the Wellington Pier was playing to full houses and the Winter Gardens were packed with visitors dancing to Maurice Illife's Broadcasting Band, audiences at the Marina were small.

> Deserving for more support than it has received up to the present is the Municipal Orchestra at the Marina. Here there are 26 musicians conducted by Mr G Francis providing light musical fare ideally suited for the idle holiday hours.[5]

It would seem that the majority of Great Yarmouth's holidaymakers were seeking something more modern and entertaining than that provided by the Municipal Orchestra. Its backward looking musical style had limited appeal; a style amply illustrated by the programme of music contained in the BBC broadcast by the orchestra on 10 August 1946 which included Paso Doble music from Frederic Charrosin's *Don Jose*; *Song D'Autumne* by the English waltz king Archibold Joyce; the humoresque *Perpétuum Morale* and *Musikalischer Scherz* by Richard Strauss II; Leslie Bridgemeon's serenade *Moonlight over Tahiti* and melodies from Schubert's *Lilac Time*.

While the creation of a Municipal Orchestra was approved of by many and filled a definite gap in the town's own musical offerings, it became apparent that its appeal was to a minority and not to the tastes of the majority of visitors to the town, especially the younger visitors. Consequently, it proved not to be the most appropriate choice of music for a seafront entertainment.

> Sir – I would like to ask whether those responsible for providing summer entertainment in the town are thoroughly versed in the wants of visitors if they have not been in the amusement world, they know little about it, for it takes most of a lifetime to be thoroughly conversant with the changing tastes of the public. The seaside today has become a great show business, for visitors do not come for sands and ozone alone. They want to be amused as well and will select the resort with the most attractions and novelty. Do those responsible think there is any novelty in the name 'Municipal Orchestra'? The town has no such fame as the South Coast resorts and is starting where others have finished. This orchestra contains no novelty for average members of the younger generations.[6]

Neither was the weather-affected Marina an ideal venue for a 26 piece orchestra performing with many delicate instruments and sheet music that blew away in the breeze. During a speech made at the Friends Meeting House in August, George Francis was forced to admit that, although seaside orchestras had not had their day, a concert orchestra at the Marina would never succeed because it was a venue open to the elements. He confirmed that many performances had been badly affected by wet weather and suggested that it had been a mistake not to have given the Marina a roof when it was first constructed. For the second year running, a thunder storm on August Bank Holiday Monday had interrupted the afternoon's concert performance. To avoid any problems with the weather, all the Municipal Orchestra's broadcasts for the BBC were made from inside the Wellington Pier Pavilion Theatre rather than from the roofless Marina. All these problems led to the Marina making a financial loss over the summer season and ensured that a Municipal Orchestra on the seafront was an experiment never to be repeated.

Reflecting on the difficulties experienced during the recently ended summer season at the September Committee meeting, Councillor Winterburn voiced the growing opinion that the Marina would continue to lose money until it was roofed over and provided entertainments that had a greater appeal to the visiting public. An inquiry was subsequently initiated instructing the Borough Engineer to look into the possibility of providing a roof and to improve the versatility of the Marina. In May 1947, Councillor Chittleburgh, chairman of the newly-merged Entertainments and Publicity Committee commented:

> Last year we tried something which I liked very much – a municipal orchestra. It was a loss and in my opinion it is hopeless to give that type of entertainment in the Marina which has not a roof. When it has a roof, and plans have been made, although it may be some time before something is done, I would like to see the floor levelled and then we would have the ideal place for a circular roller skating drome, for boxing tournaments and for a centrally heated conference hall. [7]

as well as a facility for musical concerts and dances. There was even a suggestion that it could be converted into a Lido. Until such a time that a roof was built, it was agreed that entertainment at the Marina for the 1947 and subsequent summer seasons should return to the traditional format of a dance band concert and variety show.

Efforts to provide Great Yarmouth with its own municipal orchestra continued unabated and a concert orchestra was successfully reformed in 1950 under the leadership of Maurice Illife, a retired local bandleader. The 40-strong orchestra gave regular concerts during the summer season from the Town Hall ballroom. However, musical tastes were gradually changing, audiences declined and the orchestra was disbanded in 1951. Maurice Illife was born in Leicester and, with the encouragement of his family, became a proficient performer on piano and trombone. He became a professional musician when he joined the Leicester based Ritz Players in 1926, performing seasons with the band as far afield as Jersey, Birmingham and at the Piccadilly Hotel in the West End of London. In 1932 he became leader of the Ritz Players, and in 1937 brought the band to Great Yarmouth where they became the resident dance band of the ballroom at the Wellington Pier Winter Gardens. The Ritz Players were regular performers on BBC radio and became the first band to broadcast live from Great Yarmouth. In 1942 he formed his own orchestra which became the resident dance band at the Winter Gardens from the end of World War Two until 1949, when he retired to become a publican at the Bridge Hotel in Southtown. He was for a long time musical director of the Great Yarmouth Operatic and Dramatic Society, and in 1950 helped to found the short-lived Great Yarmouth Concert Orchestra. Maurice Illife died at his home in Ormesby in 1979.[8]

---

1 Yarmouth Mercury, 21 April 1945.
2 *Ibid.*, 9 February 1946.
3 *Ibid.*, 9 February 1946.
4 *Ibid.*, 6 July 1946.
5 *Ibid.*, 27 July 1946.
6 *Ibid.*, 3 August 1946 - Letters to the Editor.
7 *Ibid.*, 7 May 1947.
8 *Ibid.*, 7 September 1979.

11. An empty Marina and a proliferation of jackets, overcoats and mackintoshes suggest that this 1951 photograph of the Marine Parade was taken on a chilly Sunday morning in Great Yarmouth. Yet the Parade is busy with visitors and the horse drawn carriage is doing good business. (Archant)

12. The 1950s were the best days for Great Yarmouth as a holiday destination. Neville Bishop's show Music on Parade attracted big audiences to the Marina. (NCC/YL)

4

High Days and Holidays

Having made the decision to return to a variety show, the Entertainments Committee invited the band leader Neville Bishop, through his promoter Catlin's Productions, to provide holiday entertainments at the Marina similar to those which he had successfully inaugurated in 1938. The invitation having been accepted with some alacrity, Neville Bishop and his 15 piece band were formally engaged to organise the entertainment at the Marina and the Floral Hall in Gorleston for the 1947 summer season from 14 June until 6 September at £400 a week. The proposals that he presented to the Committee asserted his faith in the style of entertainment that he and Richard Courtney had initiated at the Marina before the outbreak of war; a format that was unanimously adopted and which subsequently became the norm for some years to come. A morning show for children hosted by the resident band leader, and afternoon and evening shows of music and comedy aimed at adults and involving music with a balance between classical pieces, well known standards and current popular songs; all interspersed with novelty numbers. Every show was to contain comedy sketches and competitions, both serious and frivolous, involving the audience where possible – from seriously competitive talent, bathing beauty and personality competitions to the less competitive search for the bonniest baby or the man with the knobbiest knees.

13. *A publicity photograph of Neville Bishop's 1948 Band with each member identified by his autograph. Part of the Arnold Rack collection.* (AR)

As a result, the 1947 summer season was great success compared with that of 1946. The Marina made a profit and Neville Bishop and his band were re-engaged for 1948. Audiences appeared to be willing to make exhibitions of themselves in the many games and competitions, some of which occasionally revealed undiscovered talents in the most unprepossessing members of the public. The weekly bathing beauty competition drew contestants from all over the country. The band, with its signature tune *Who's Afraid of the Big Bad Wolf*, demonstrated versatility and skill, and often had the whole audience participating in novelty songs like the popular *Bobbing Up and Down* or miming

14. *A letter from the Premier Drum Company to drummer Arnold Rack at the Marina regarding the purchase of musical instruments. H. Morris from the Sales Department thanks Rack for the present of nylon stockings which were definitely in short supply in 1947.* (AR)

15. A 1948 version of the Mexican Hat Dance? (AR)

to *One Finger, One Thumb Keep Moving.* The star of the show was always Neville Bishop who regularly brought the house down with his jazz style drumming on a drum set comprised of kitchen pots and pans.

Neville Bishop was born in Kingston-upon-Thames, the only son of Mr and Mrs William Bishop, who were both leading figures in the entertainments business. His father was an internationally known theatrical producer and his Kings Lynn-born mother had appeared on the stage in many West End and Broadway musicals. When he retired from the stage, his father bought a chain of hotels in London and Margate, and, at 18 years of age, Neville was sent to the Ritz Hotel in Paris to learn kitchen management in the hope that he would develop as an hotelier. But music was his first love and he was intent upon becoming a drummer. In Paris, he frequently entertained his fellow workers with drum solos on the pots and pans in the kitchen, a skill that he later incorporated into his musical repertoire as a novelty item. Determined upon a musical career, he left home and eventually gained employment as a drummer with the Bert Ambrose Orchestra and then with Jack Hylton. Under Jack Hylton's patronage, he was encouraged to form his own band and spent seven years touring with them throughout the Continent playing American jazz style dance band music. On his return to Britain, he became the resident band leader at the Trianon Club in London and at the Marina in Great Yarmouth for the 1938 and 1939 summer seasons. During the war, he joined ENSA and obtained a posting with the 1ˢᵗ Canadian Army performing in their front-line band show, *Follow the Drum*. After the war, he formed a new band, Neville Bishop and his Wolves, and spent most of his working life appearing in summer season shows, mainly in Great Yarmouth at the Marina (1947-48 and 1956–59), the Floral Hall and the Britannia Pier. His Scottish-born wife was formerly his pianist. In 1960 he retired to manage the Anchor Hotel in Thetford.[1]

Surprisingly, the contract to supply the entertainment at the Marina for the 1949 summer season was won by the promoter Frederick Hargreaves on behalf of Ronnie Mills and his Orchestra. For the next three years, Ronnie Mills appeared at the Marina in performances of *Summer Serenade* and *Bandshow of 1950* and *1951* at a cost of £325 a week, following closely the successful format that had been introduced by Neville Bishop. Neville Bishop's association with Great Yarmouth did not cease with the loss of the Marina contract as he was subsequently engaged to perform as the resident band at the Britannia Pier theatre.

Public school educated, ex-guardsman Ronnie Mills was formerly the leading trumpeter with Edmundo Ross' orchestra. Following in the tradition of Edmundo Ross, Ronnie Mills' Orchestra played music in a gentle manner and provided backing for baritone Roy Taylor, a crooner in the style of Bing Crosby, formerly with the Squadronaires, and soprano Audrey Desmond. Comedy was provided by Jim Fitz and Carl Lloyd. Every performance featured a competition of one form or another, including weekly heats for the *Miss Yarmouth* bathing beauty title and the *Search for a Star* amateur talent competition. Prizes were modest but included a pair of nylon stockings every evening, a much sought-after commodity in 1950.

In 1952, Ronnie Mills was himself replaced by the long established and well-known Waldini and his Gypsy Band in the musical show *Music with a Smile* and again in 1953 as *Showband of 1953*. Waldini, the stage name of Wallace Bishop from Cardiff, had performed with his orchestra in most seaside resorts since the 1920s, arriving in Great

Frederic Hargroves presents RONNIE MILLS AND HIS ORCHESTRA The Marina, YARMOUTH.

16. *A 1949 publicity photograph for Ronnie Mills' Orchestra. Bow ties were a must. The debonair ex-guardsman Ronnie Mills is on the right and singers Roy Taylor and Audrey Desmond stand to the left.*

Yarmouth after three successful seasons in Southport. During the war, Waldini had joined ENSA and was reputed to have played in 23 different countries during four and a half years of service. Playing in a gypsy manner, his orchestra featured violins and accordions. Fronting the band was singer Nanw Morgan, the Welsh Nightingale, and comedy was again provided by the Lancashire comedian Jimmy Fitz who had formerly appeared with Ronnie Mills. Sunday concerts were given by the locally-based Bert Galley and his Orchestra with a special appearance by the nationally popular Dagenham Girl Pipers on Sunday 2 August.

Tastes were changing, particularly among young people, and audience numbers fell. Replacing the heats of the *Miss Yarmouth* bathing beauty competition with a personality girl competition proved unpopular and, together with long periods of unsettled weather, resulted in low attendance figures.

I have just returned to Scotland from my first visit to Yarmouth and had it not been for Waldini's very fine orchestra my visit would have been very dull. Why do the people of Yarmouth not appreciate good music and musicians at a very good night's entertainment? Why is the Marina not filled to capacity at every performance? Is it because they prefer a juke box? May I say thank you to Waldini and his orchestra for making my holiday most enjoyable.[2]

Nevertheless, Waldini's gypsy style of music was considered too old fashioned for audiences strongly attracted to jazz, crooners and the big band sound from America.

In an attempt to rectify falling audience numbers at the Marina, the council decided to appoint a nationally known artist for the 1954 season and after some deliberation successfully engaged the services of Harry Hudson and his band, the Melody Boys. Harry Hudson was well-known to most audiences of the 1950s because, in 1953, he had replaced Violet Carson as the resident pianist for Wilfred Pickles on the BBC's first radio quiz game, *Have a Go*. Born in 1898, Hudson began his musical career in music hall as a singer and pianist. In 1928 he became musical director for the Edison Bell record label and formed a studio orchestra

17. *Informality and pullovers were the order of the day for Harry Hudson and his Melody Boys on this 1954 publicity photograph. In 1953, Hudson took over from Violet Carson as the resident pianist on Wilfred Pickles' radio show 'Have a Go'.*

that produced cheap records under various pseudonyms. For the 1954 summer season at Great Yarmouth, he gathered together a number of talented singers and musicians including accordionist Warwick Bidgood and xylophonist Dorothy Marno.

Warwick Bidgood came from a large musical family. His father, Thomas Bidgood was famous for composing the popular song *Sons of the Brave* while his pianist brother Harry, under the name Primo Scala, formed the famous Primo Scala's Accordion Band and appeared regularly on BBC Radio's *Music While You Work* as well as providing the musical score for various George Formby films including *It Turned Out Nice Again, Come on George* and *Let George Do It*. Warwick Bidgood was chief accordionist in his brother's band and it was possibly the influence of Norfolk-based George Formby that led to Warwick's inclusion in Hudson's band. Dorothy Marno was a well-known xylophonist, famous throughout the 1930s for heading her own ladies-only jazz band. As well as band music, Hudson, with Roy Stewart, performed in a duet act playing classical and popular melodies on two pianos.

Introduced by the signature tune *I'm just wild about Harry*, Hudson encouraged his audiences to join in and sing, and taught them the words to his composition *Dear Old Yarmouth by the Sea*.

Happy Days are holidays
At dear old Yarmouth by the sea,
Take your gals, meet your pals
Join in the fun and harmony
Fathers, mothers, young and old
Are kids again
Just one big fam-i-ly
Happy days are holidays
At dear old Yarmouth by the sea.

For the 1955 season, the Council once again turned to the old stalwart, Neville Bishop and his band, the Wolves, to revitalise the entertainment at the Marina. This he did with a vengeance and for the next five years, with Bishop in control, the Marina became one of the most popular attractions on the Promenade. The years from 1955 until 1959 were the Marina's heyday, just as they were also for Great

18. *The colourful McNamara's Band. At every performance the band would march around the auditorium led by Neville Bishop brandishing a mop.*

Yarmouth as a seaside holiday resort. Bishop's infectious enthusiasm together with a well-tried weekly programme in the manner of Billy Cotton, combining music of all styles with slapstick comedy, ensured that on fine summer days the band played to full houses. Saxophonist Sonny Lee noted that:

> The type of music the boys have to play varies considerably. Moments after accompanying an operatic aria it's quite on the cards that they will be up-tempoing (sic) their merry way through a big-band version of *Hamp's Boogie*. Dixieland might well follow Ketelby's *In a Monastery Garden*, hit parade "pops" give way to riotous arrangements of *Knees up Mother Brown* and *Old MacDonald had a Farm*.[3]

The Yarmouth Mercury correspondent Peggotty in his weekly *Yarmouth Porthole* also nostalgically commented:

> I remember Neville Bishop, garbed in bathrobe and carrying a mop, leading the musicians as they marched around the Marina audience, where every child flocked to follow as if he were the Pied Piper himself. Out they went on to Marine

Parade and back again, this time with far more followers than when they left. It was a great advertisement for the place.[4]

The weekly programme produced by Bishop and his band ensured a different offering for every day of the week. Holidaymakers could visit the Marina each day in the week and not see the same show twice. Even the three daily performances in the morning, afternoon and evening were different. The morning show was aimed primarily at children and their parents; the afternoon was a show for all ages while the evening show was mainly intended for adults. Every morning at 11.00am, *Uncle Neville's Happy-go-Lucky Party* included a Children's Talent contest together with games and competitions; skipping contests, Best Looking Boy, Best Girl's Hairstyle and Best Fancy Dress for the children, a knitting race for the mothers and a Fastest Ice-cream Eating contest for the dads. The best performers at each day's talent contest were paraded out again at a Grand Final during the Friday afternoon show. Afternoon and evening shows throughout the week also included an Adult Talent Competition with a Grand Final on Friday evening. The winners were decided by audience applause and certificates and prizes were given to the best acts.

19. *Programme cover from the 1959 entertainment, 'This is Your Show'.*

Saturday's shows were designated as *Time to meet the Band*, an opportunity for newly arrived visitors to sample what was on offer throughout the week at the Marina. The Sunday shows provided a more subdued offering called *Sunday Serenade*, less frenetic so as not to offend those who still observed the Sabbath Day. The evening show was normally entitled *Anniversary Night* and celebrated any couple in the audience with a wedding anniversary during their stay in Great Yarmouth. Competitions on Sundays included a search for *The Best Old*

20. *In 1959, holidaymakers could see a different programme every day of the week at the Marina.*

Couple over 65' and an invitation to conduct the band. On Mondays, the two shows targeted young people; in the afternoon a sponsored search for the young woman with the best personality, variously called *Miss Exquisite Form* and *Miss Babycham Holiday Girl*; in the evening a dance competition for young couples performing jive, rock 'n' roll or the cha cha. Tuesday's shows were for everybody; the afternoon targeted all the family while the evening was *Father's Night*, during which the dads were subjected to various humiliations such as *Dress up Father* and *Giving Father a Close Shave*. Wednesday's shows included the preliminary rounds for the adult talent contest while every Thursday the popular attraction was a heat for the *Miss Yarmouth* bathing beauty contest with the final usually at the end of August; Fridays concluded the week with the finals for the kiddies and adult talent contests before the weekly round began again on the Saturday.

The Yarmouth March, performed at the Marina's opening ceremony in 1937, and *Dear old Yarmouth by the Sea* were not the only musical pieces composed to celebrate Great Yarmouth's position as a premier holiday resort. In 1956 Ronnie Ronalde, backed by the Great Yarmouth Town Council, released a recording of a composition entitled *The Yarmouth Song*; a simple catchy tune designed to appeal to the general public but, realistically, a song whose lyrics did little to promote the real benefits of a holiday by the sea.

One, two, three, jolly good company,
in wonderful Yarmouth by the sea.
Yarmouth, wonderful Yarmouth,
the place that has everything,
Yarmouth, wonderful Yarmouth,
you'll be as happy as a king.

Strolling down the lovely promenade,
your worries disappear and life is not
so hard.
Pretty girls all out upon the spree,
Give them a hug, give them a
squeeze,
and take them on your knee.

In Yarmouth, wonderful Yarmouth,
lift your voices merrily,
One, two, three, jolly good company,
in wonderful Yarmouth by the sea.

Use your smart phone or tablet to scan this QR code and hear Ronnie Ronalde's 1956 rendition of 'The Yarmouth Song' re-released by EMI in 2001 and provided on YouTube by the Warner Music Group in 2017.

In the early 1950s, Ronnie Ronalde, the popular whistler, singer and yodeller, was a regular summertime performer in Great Yarmouth's seaside theatres. In 1951, he appeared in *Meet the Stars* with Max Bygraves at the Britannia Pier, and returned again for the 1955 and 1956 seasons to star in *The Ronnie Ronalde Show* at the council-owned Wellington Pier. It was during one of his 1956 shows that Ronnie Ronalde performed *The Yarmouth Song* in public for the very first time.

Ronnie Ronalde was born Ronald Charles Waldron at Islington, London in 1923. His talent for singing, whistling and bird song impressions was soon recognised and in 1938, at the age of 15, he was invited to join Steffani's Silver Songsters, a popular professional choir for boys that was managed and conducted by Arturo Steffani, the adopted stage name of Frederick William Wisker from Beccles. Through singing in the choir he performed in theatres throughout the United Kingdom, made recordings for Decca and appeared regularly on

BBC radio. In 1947, the Silver Songsters were disbanded and having recognised Ronald Waldron's exceptional talent, Steffani became Ronald's manager, changing Waldron's name to Ronnie Ronalde, heralding the beginning of a successful business partnership that continued into the 1960s. Ronalde, as he was called thereafter, reached the height of his popularity in the early 1950s when he was well-known for his recordings of *If I were a Blackbird*, *Bells across the Meadow* and *In a Monastery Garden*, compositions that displayed perfectly his talent for singing as well as for whistling.

The Yarmouth Song was composed specifically for Ronalde by his manager Arturo Steffani as a celebration of their happy and successful seasons in Great Yarmouth. In due course, Ronalde's rendition of the song was recorded by Columbia Records[5] and released in the summer of 1956 with his version of *Macnamara's Band*, the new signature tune of the Marina's resident band, Neville Bishop and his Wolves, as the B side. Having been adopted by the Great Yarmouth Town Council as the resort's official publicity song, copies of both the record and its sheet music were sold through council-owned kiosks at the Wellington Pier and the Marina. Unfortunately, in 1956, tastes in popular music were changing. Bill Haley and Elvis Presley were establishing new styles in music and, as the traditional music-hall sound of *The Yarmouth Song* failed to appeal to the public, particularly the teenage public, sales of the recording were poor. In 1957, the Great Yarmouth Town Council ceased promoting the record and requested that Ronalde and Steffani should remove the remaining unsold copies that were being stored on their behalf at the Marina.

In the 1960s, Ronnie Ronalde moved to Guernsey with his Austrian wife, Rosemarie, where he managed the successful Ronnie Ronalde Hotel for the next 20 years as well as continuing to make regular broadcast and concert appearances. In the 1980s, after a short stay on the Isle of Man, he moved with his family to New Zealand before finally settling in Queensland, Australia, where he continued to be popular as a performer and entertainer. *The Yarmouth Song* remained part of his musical repertoire and was adopted as the theme tune for the town of Yarmouth in Australia. Ronalde's recording of *The Yarmouth Song* was re-issued on the CD, *The Magic of Ronnie Ronalde*, which was released by EMI in 2001[6].

All attempts to develop the Marina as a conference centre were destined to fail mainly because the lack of a roof and any form of heating restricted the use of the facility to the warmer and drier summer months. In the winter the Marina was used simply as a storehouse for deckchairs, kiosks and any other council-owned beach furniture that was used by council employees during the holiday season, as well as housing two or three privately-owned motorboats that were used in the summer to convey adventurous visitors over the water to see the seals on Scroby Sands. Little attempt was made to promote the Marina as a conference centre following severe criticism of the facility after a British Legion conference was held there in 1949.

Nevertheless, various attempts were made to vary the type of entertainment on offer. In 1947, an open-air boxing tournament was arranged by a Yarmouth based promoter, Dick Turner. On Tuesday 12 June, an audience of over 2,000 people at the Marina witnessed the first ever professional open-air event of this type held in Great Yarmouth. The tournament, consisting of six bouts, featured local Lowestoft-born Mickey Thompson against Johnny Cunningham from London as the top-of-the-bill contest. Thompson won a close fought match and subsequently went on to challenge Keith Weston for the Eastern Area welterweight title.

In response to a number of Government initiatives regarding the wellbeing of senior members in society, on Wednesday 7 June 1950 the first Norfolk County Old Folks' Clubs' Rally was held at the Marina, organised by the Norfolk Welfare Committee. The Marina was chosen as the venue for the rally as it was the only place available in Norfolk that could cope with the number of old people attending; over 4,000 from 42 old people's clubs throughout the county. On a fine Wednesday afternoon, entertainment was provided by Ronnie Mills and his Orchestra.

> Programmes, pocket handkerchiefs and a hat on the end
> of a stick were waved as Mr Arthur Caiger, who led the

singing at the Wembley Cup Final, led half-an-hour of community singing. Ballads that were popular at the turn of the century were sung by Nora Germaine, John Grey & Bobby Bent and later the old people joined in a hilarious version of *I've got a Lovely Bunch of Coconuts* when four veteran volunteers sung solos and ended by prancing round the Marina in feathered hats followed by the band. [7]

21. *From 1950, the annual Norfolk County Old Folks Club's Rally was held at the Marina. Members of the audience were not shy of joining the band on stage to play games, sing songs or take part in hilarious competitions. (Archant)*

The success of the first rally ensured that the Marina became the location for all subsequent rallies for the next ten years. The formula that was begun in 1950 was repeated again in 1951:

The response to Mr Arthur Caiger, who conducted the community singing during the afternoon's concert, could hardly have been more whole-hearted as he led them through choruses ranging from *Land of Hope & Glory* to *I do Like to be Beside the Seaside* and *John Brown's Body*. Two old age pensioners, Mr Lake from Sprowston and Mrs Brunsen, each volunteered to sing a verse of *Cockles and Mussels* as a solo and the rousing choruses were sung by the rest of the large gathering. There was likewise no reticence about joining Ronnie Mills who, with his band and artists, entertained the old folks during the afternoon.[8]

By 1955 audiences had risen to 4,500 drawn from over 95 clubs throughout Norfolk. Not even bad weather could dampen their spirits.

Rain during lunchtime caused some rearrangement of plans and eventually only those people under cover remained at the Marina, the rest being entertained by Ronnie in the Winter Gardens Ballroom and by members of the *Showtime* company in the Wellington Pier Pavilion. Many drivers stopped their cars outside the Marina on seeing people unable to walk gathering there and took them to the Wellington pier. One car, with a number of young holiday-makers inside, drew up when they saw what was happening and all the occupants except the driver got out in the rain to make room for some more of the infirm.[9]

By the end of the decade, attendance dropped to around 2,000, possibly as a result of improved television provision throughout the county, and from 1962 the rally was transferred to the Floral Hall.

---

1   Yarmouth Mercury, 23 July 1948.
2   *Ibid.*, 15 July 1952.
3   Eastern Evening News, 26 May 1956.
4   *Ibid. 1*, 10 February 1979.
5   Columbia DB3768. *The Yarmouth Song/Macnamara's Band*.
6   EMI CD724353189228 *The Magic of Ronnie Ronalde* 16 April 2001.
7   *Ibid. 1*, 9 June 1950.
8   *Ibid.*, 15 June 1951.
9   *Ibid.*, 19 June 1953.

Give

for

those

who

Gave

Thousands of our finest men and women in the Royal Air Forces have given their service, their health, and in many cases their lives, for their Country and in defence of Freedom. Today many of them, and their dependants, are in urgent need of the R.A.F. Association's Welfare Service. Please give all you can for your emblem on Wings Day *or send a donation direct to Headquarters.*

WEAR THIS EMBLEM ON SATURDAY

WINGS DAY

SATURDAY, SEPTEMBER 20th

ROYAL AIR FORCES ASSOCIATION

Registered under the War Charities Act, 1940 83 Portland Place, W.1

PROCEEDS TO BE DEVOTED TO CHARITABLE AND WELFARE PURPOSES

239.20B

22. Wings Day street collections for the RAFA Benevolent Fund were held each year on the Saturday closest to the 15 September.

5

Great Yarmouth's Battle of Britain Celebrations

In March 1946, the Great Yarmouth & Gorleston branch of the Royal Air Forces Association (RAFA) applied to the Town Council's Entertainment Committee for the use of council-owned facilities to house fund raising activities on Saturday 14 September during Battle of Britain weekend; a request to which the Council was more than happy to accede. As a consequence, Great Yarmouth's first Battle of Britain commemorative festival was held consisting of a bathing beauty contest at the Marina in the morning, a carnival parade through the town and a RAF flypast in the afternoon. A Victory Ball was held at the Wellington Pier Winter Gardens in the evening. The tradition of a special Battle of Britain memorial day began in 1943 when King George VI approved Sunday 26 September as a day for celebrating victory in the World War Two air battle fought in the skies over southern England during the summer and autumn of 1940. The tradition continued after the war when, as *Flight Magazine* announced:

> Churches of all denominations have authorised collections to be taken on Battle of Britain Sunday (September 15 1946) for the RAF Benevolent Fund."[1]

The 15th of September 1940 was a particularly successful day for the Royal Air Force. It was considered by many to be the point at which the Luftwaffe accepted that they could not win and the planned German invasion of Britain was put on hold. After the war, RAFA initiated a national festival of activities and entertainments during September around Battle of Britain Sunday to raise money for the RAF Benevolent Fund; a charitable fund for assisting ex-RAF servicemen and their families in need. Included in these activities was a flag day with street collections for the Benevolent Fund on the Saturday closest to 15 September entitled Wings Day.

Traditionally, Great Yarmouth's summer season began on the Whitsun (now late May) Bank Holiday weekend and ended with the late September flat-race meeting at the Caister Road racecourse. Attracting visitors outside the peak holiday months of July and August was a major concern for the Town Council. To encourage more visitors, activities during the first and last few weeks of the summer season regularly targeted the retired and handicapped members of the public. Before World War Two, the council had also considered organising a late summer festival week to attract day visitors as well as holidaymakers. Consequently, the Battle of Britain celebrations were considered to be a most welcome addition to the late summer programme of events and RAFA received full cooperation from the Town Council.

By 1950, the festival in Great Yarmouth had grown to become a well-established and popular annual event called Battle of Britain Week, covering 10 or more days of activities including a beauty contest and fancy dress competitions at the Marina, a swimming gala at the pool, whist drives, dances and a bowls tournament on the Marina bowling greens. The week sometimes included a grand carnival procession through the town, although the proceeds raised during this event were not always dedicated solely to the benevolent fund. In 1947 part of the proceeds from the procession were donated to the Great Yarmouth Hospital Fund and at other times money was raised for the RNLI and the St Nicholas Church Restoration Fund.

Neither a Battle of Britain Festival Week nor a carnival procession was a new idea. Hospital Days that included a carnival procession as part of the organised activities were an annual summertime feature in Great Yarmouth and Gorleston during the 1930s, raising funds for their respective hospitals. Great Yarmouth's Hospital Day was held on the Thursday of August Bank Holiday Week, then the first full week in August, and Gorleston's Hospital Day a week later. Contributions from these fund raising activities were essential to balancing the books for both hospitals. In 1936, the organisers of Great Yarmouth's Hospital Day planned to raise £1,200 as the hospital was over £900 in debt. As well as assisting with the day to day finances of its cottage hospital, the surplus proceeds from Gorleston's Hospital Day contributed towards the £45,000 needed to build a new hospital in the grounds of the Grange on Lowestoft Road. A feature of both hospital days was the help given with the street collections by the 'Gari boys', 800 or so young men holidaying in bachelor apartments at the Garibaldi Hotel in Great Yarmouth, their imaginative fancy dress providing a colourful contribution to the day's carnival atmosphere. With the outbreak of war, carnival processions were banned and the Yarmouth and Gorleston Hospital Day activities were reduced to joint fund-raising fetes held at the Wellesley sports stadium or in the grounds of the Northgate Road Hospital.

Between the two World Wars, three week-long midsummer festivals were also held in the hope of attracting visitors to the town. The first two took place in 1922 and 1923 in an attempt to provide a temporary escape from the hard times and economic depression experienced as a consequence of World War One and the subsequent disastrous Spanish flu pandemic of 1918, as well as to revive the holiday industry in Great Yarmouth. The carnival of 1923 included a re-enactment of Lord Nelson's landing at the jetty after the Battle of Copenhagen when he received the freedom of the borough at the Wrestlers Inn on Church Plain. The re-enactment included a carnival procession that was hailed as being one of the finest spectacles ever seen in the town.

> No more brilliant spectacle has ever been witnessed in the borough than the procession of decorated motor vehicles, trade vehicles, commercial tableaux and humorous turnouts, which took place on Thursday afternoon......

The procession was led by mounted police followed by the Municipal Military Band and King Carnival, his retinue and body guards followed, and then the order was the Mayor and the Town Clerk and Organising Secretary, the Mayoress and party, No 1 Fire Engine, Father Neptune and his mermaids, Nelson's carriage with Lord Nelson, the Mayor of Tunbridge, the handfly in which rode Lady Hamilton, Aldermen and councillors of Nelson's period, citizens and citizenesses of Nelson's day. The sedan chair was mounted on a lorry, and then came the old fish cart. Decorated private cars and trade vehicles, commercial tableaux, pony and donkey turn-outs were next in order, and finally the lifeboat brought the rear.[2]

The week's other activities included a sports meeting and gymkhana at the Wellesley, a swimming gala, golf, cricket and bowls tournaments, concerts and dances, firework displays from the Britannia Pier and a swimming race between the Britannia and Wellington Piers for the Ulph Challenge Cup. The race was first swum on Thursday 15 September 1887 for a prize of 10 guineas and a silver medal, and in September every year thereafter for a cup presented by Mr H. Ulph of the Great Yarmouth Swimming Club.

Due to the depressed economic circumstances of the early 1930s, visitor numbers dropped and so, in 1933, the Publicity Committee considered the possibility of a third carnival week to revive the flagging fortunes of Great Yarmouth's holiday industry. Although the earlier carnivals were considered to have been a great success there was a reluctance on the part of some committee members to agree to another festival. It was felt that retailers, especially those in the centre of town, had benefited little from the carnivals and that the only people profiting from the influx of tourists were caterers, innkeepers and purveyors of carnival novelties. The fact that most of Great Yarmouth's holiday attractions were closed on Sundays was also considered to be a deterrent to weekend visitors. Nevertheless, a third carnival was planned and took place from 2 until 6 July 1934. In an attempt to outdo the carnival of 1923, the entertainments included historical pageants depicting the

23. The 1934 Carnival Procession passes the Queen's Hotel. England lost the 1934 Ashes series. Australia clinched a 2 - 1 victory with a first innings score of 701 in the final deciding fifth test at the Oval. As indicated by the scoreboard, Players cigarettes were 10 for sixpence (2½p).

visits to the town by King Richard II and King William III. A fourth summertime carnival week planned for July 1935 was cancelled and replaced by a festival in May to celebrate the Jubilee of King George V and Queen Mary. No further carnival weeks were considered and it seems that the Council thereafter focused its efforts on promoting the newly constructed Marina as the town's prime holiday attraction.

During the 1950s and early 1960s, Battle of Britain Week was an extremely well supported festival and many of the week's activities were held at the Marina, the most popular of which were the bathing beauty contest, Bonnie Baby and children's fancy dress competitions and the dancing displays by Jean Boulton's School of Dancing.

> With over 2,000 spectators and 56 entrants, the children's fancy dress contest at the Marina on Wednesday afternoon proved the most successful competition of its kind to be arranged by the RAF Association. There was a wide variety of costumes among the children whose ages ranged from 18 months to about 13 years. The prize for the best comical dress went to children from Caister Holiday Camp who

appeared as the Bash Street Kids.[3]

The crowning of the carnival king was also held at the Marina. In 1950, the Yarmouth Mercury reported that:

> King Carnival was crowned with due ceremony at the Marina on Monday afternoon. The way was prepared and the atmosphere created for the royal entry by Ronnie Mills and his orchestra. Then, to a fanfare of trumpets, the King and his court jesters entered the Marina. The procession of jesters, courtiers, ministers of state, pages and rejoicing crowd moved up to the stage where the King, Ted Gatty of the *Hilarity* company from Gorleston Pavilion, regally ascended his throne. A Queen Carnival was quickly called for but the dark-eyed, dark chinned, "raven-haired beauty" that appeared was even more quickly dismissed. After the usual preliminaries the King was duly crowned whereupon he insisted on knighting that master of music, Ronnie Mills. Finally, the King and his court made a triumphant exit led by "Sir Ronnie Mills" and his orchestra to the strains of *I've got a Lovely Bunch of Coconuts*.[4]

In March 1946 as part of its plans for Wings Day, the Great Yarmouth branch of RAFA submitted a request to the town's Entertainments Committee for a venue to hold a beauty contest in the coming September. The resulting bathing beauty competition that was held at the Marina on the morning of Saturday 14 September 1946 as part of the town's Battle of Britain celebrations was the first in an unbroken 25 year sequence of contests to elect Great Yarmouth's *Miss Battle of Britain* during the late summer remembrance festival. The competition judge chosen for the occasion was Norman Pett, creator of the Daily Mirror's cartoon pin-up, Jane. An appropriate selection as Jane, the scantily dressed adventuress who featured in the Daily Mirror's 'Cartoon strip that Teased', was a firm favourite with British troops during World War Two. Of the 38 young women who entered the competition, 32 were resident in the Great Yarmouth area. Nevertheless, the eventual winner of *Miss Battle of Britain* 1946 was 27 year old Hazel Gay, from Wallington in Surrey, who was appearing as a dancer in the summer production of *Showtime* at the Wellington Pier Pavilion. The prizes were modest and for winning the contest Miss Gay was rewarded with the princely sum of £35. Thereafter, every September until 1970, a bathing beauty competition was held for the title of *Miss Battle of Britain*, mostly at the Marina. In addition to receiving a money prize and gifts, the winner was expected to perform various ceremonial duties during the resort's Battle of Britain Week, including attending at formal dances and leading the carnival procession in the role of carnival queen. As well as assuming the title of *Miss Battle of Britain*, she was also declared *Miss RAFA Great Yarmouth* and given an automatic entry into the national *Miss RAFA* competition.

The one exemption to this rule occurred in 1947 when separate competitions were held for the *Miss Battle of Britain* and *Miss RAFA* titles, the former at the Wellington Pier Pavilion and the latter at the Marina. The reason for this separation was because the carnival procession held during the 1947 remembrance festival raised funds for Great Yarmouth's hospital and not for the RAF Benevolent Fund - the last year in which such fund raising was necessary before the establishment of the National Health Service. That year, the *Miss RAFA* 1947 title, a competition to discover the prettiest WAAF or ex-WAAF, was won by Daphne Munford, who received a cake stand as her prize. In good weather, the outdoor nature of the Marina theatre provided an ideal setting for these bathing beauty contests. However, the vagaries of the British weather, especially in September, meant that some competitions were badly affected by wind and rain, a factor that partly contributed to their eventual demise.

Great Yarmouth's Battle of Britain Bathing Beauty contest was traditionally held on the first day of the resort's annual Battle of Britain celebrations. Other than during the years 1947 to 1952, the contest took place in the Marina and continued to be held there without a break until 1970, when it was abandoned. The format for the contest varied little during the 25 years of its existence. Initially, the contestants paraded one by one across the Marina's stage, dressed in a bathing suit and holding their designated number. The show was usually compered by the leader of the Marina's resident band, who conducted a brief interview with all the competitors while they were on the stage. Finally, each contestant paraded once again across the stage and around the auditorium. The winner was chosen sometimes by a panel of judges and at other times by the audience according to the volume and duration of their applause. Following the declaration of the winner, a formal ceremony was performed in which an entertainer from one of Great Yarmouth's summertime variety shows placed a crown on the head of the winner and presented the prizes. Over the years, the crowning

24. The final act before the selection of the Battle of Britain Beauty Queen was a parade of the contestants around the Marina's auditorium for the benefit of the audience. This 1950 photograph indicates that the Marina was already showing signs of wear. (Archant)

ceremony was performed by many well-known popular personalities including Vera Lynn, Yana, Bruce Forsyth, Norman Wisdom, Harry Secombe, Ken Dodd and Frank Ifield, to mention but a few. In reporting the 1955 competition won by Marianne Hatton, the Great Yarmouth Mercury stated that:

    While the crowd was entertained by Neville Bishop and his

band, *Miss Battle of Britain* and her attendants changed into their Coronation robes. Then, in a crinoline dress of white muslin with a vivid blue cloak, Miss Hatton moved to the carved wooden chair at the centre of the stage. Then, with her attendants standing around her, she was crowned with a silver beaded crown by Miss Lynn.[5]

In the early days, prizes were modest but, by the 1960s, the prize

25. *Vera Lynn presents Marianne Hatton with the 1955 Miss Battle of Britain trophy and sash. (Archant)*

money had risen considerably in value, attracting entrants from all over the country. In 1960, Charlie Drake presented the winner, Geraldine Bartlet, with a valuable diamond necklace and matching earrings. During its lifetime, the competition not only attracted young dancers from the chorus lines of Great Yarmouth's summer shows but also many local young women proud of their good looks and others from all parts of the country hoping that their participation might bring financial rewards as well as opening the door to future career opportunities. Local winners included Sylvia King, Patricia Sewell and Mary Taylor from Great Yarmouth and June Philpot from Gorleston. The final contest took place in September 1970 after which the event was discontinued due mainly to the uncertainty regarding the Marina's future and a decline in public interest for the Battle of Britain celebrations. Mr Bruce Easter, Vice Chairman of the Yarmouth & Gorleston RAFA explained that the 1971 contest had been abandoned because:

> Attendances over the years had dwindled from 4,000 to 2,000 and with the future of the Marina unknown early in the year we came to the conclusion this year that we could not go on running at a loss. It was a big disappointment to us. But it is always a dodgy business holding it in the open air.[6]

Both the 1968 and 1969 competitions were seriously affected by rain and, as a consequence, attendances were poor.

Until 1950, a carnival procession was an integral part of Battle of Britain Week, continuing the tradition of a carnival procession established during Yarmouth's annual Hospital Day, with some of the proceeds being allotted to the hospital as well as to the benevolent fund. As in the past, it continued to be held on a Thursday, early closing day in Great Yarmouth. With the advent of the National Health Service, Hospital Days became obsolete and, as a result, for most of the 1950s no carnival procession was held at Great Yarmouth. The idea of a carnival parade during Battle of Britain Week was resurrected in 1960 after a lapse of ten years, with part of the proceeds on that occasion being donated to the St Nicholas Church restoration fund. One of the activities of the 1961 Battle of Britain Week was another grand carnival parade with some of the proceeds raised on that occasion to support the Gorleston based RNLI lifeboat, the Louise Stephens. Despite the success of these carnival parades as both a money-raiser and an enjoyable spectacle, no around town processions were held after 1962 mainly due to problems with managing local traffic along the processional route.

Of all the Battle of Britain Weeks, the one held in 1961 was the most successful. The grand opening ceremony was performed at the Marina on the afternoon of Thursday 31 August. Almost 4,000 eager spectators sat in the warm late-summer sunshine to witness the opening speeches and the Mayor of Great Yarmouth, Mr. M. Edgar Barker, declare the week's festivities begun, followed by the *Miss Battle of Britain* bathing beauty competition and a performance of the show *Blow Your Top* with music from Maurice Share and his orchestra. Guests of honour for the ceremony included Group-Captain Harold Bird-Wilson, Commanding Officer of RAF Coltishall, who was a veteran pilot from the Battle of Britain, Group-Captain D. A. Green, Commanding Officer of RAF Honington, and RAF personnel G. A. Burnett and M. Wyatt.

FRIDAY — September 8th

Children's
FANCY DRESS CONTEST

at the MARINA at 3 p.m.
Adults 1/6   Children 1/-
Children in Fancy Dress FREE
with
MAURICE SHARE AND HIS SHOWBAND
inviting you to
BLOW YOUR TOP

Our big Dance event!!
THE BATTLE OF BRITAIN
CARNIVAL BALL
at the
WINTER GARDEN BALLROOM
WELLINGTON PIER
8 p.m. to Midnight

With MAURICE SHARE and his STARNOTES ORCHESTRA

Late Transport ★ Carnival Novelties   M.C. Mr. Redvers Mann
5/- AT THE DOOR

How Sad! Two pretty butterflies were turned away from the dance because it was a Moth Ball!...

26. *Locally based Maurice Share and his Orchestra were in demand.*

Air Vice-Marshall Harold Arthur Cooper (Birdie) Bird-Wilson, was born at Prestatyn in North Wales, joined the RAF in 1937 and after training was assigned to 17 Squadron flying Hawker Hurricanes. In training he suffered serious burns and facial injuries, including the loss of his nose, when an aircraft he was flying crashed in bad weather. While recovering in hospital at East Grinstead, his face was rebuilt by the pioneering plastic surgeon Archibald McIndoe, entitling him to join McIndoe's exclusive 'Guinea-pig Club' of successfully treated patients. He re-joined his squadron in time to cover the allied retreat to Dunkirk during April and May, 1940, and then to take part in the Battle of Britain from July until September. During the battle, he recorded six 'kills' but his luck ran out when he was himself shot down on 24 September 1940 by the German ace Adolf Galland. Although his Hurricane was destroyed, he managed to bail out and landed in the Thames where he was rescued by a navy MTB, incurring further burns and numerous shrapnel wounds. After a second lengthy period in hospital, he returned once again to active service in 1941 with 254 Squadron flying Spitfires that were responsible for carrying out coastal patrols and bomber escorts. Harold Bird-Wilson was Station Commander at RAF Coltishall from June 1959 until November 1961.[7]

Music for the opening ceremony was provided by the trumpeters of the 1st East Anglian Regiment and the Ceremonial Band from RAF Henlow under its musical director Flight-Lieutenant V. H. Hutchinson. In his opening speech the Mayor congratulated the members of Great Yarmouth & Gorleston RAFA for their achievement in winning the 1960 Battle of Britain Trophy and for their considerable efforts on behalf of the benevolent fund. Group-Captain Green then presented a newly-inaugurated cup that was to be awarded to the activity in the eastern division of RAFA that showed the largest percentage increase on its previous year's takings. The trophy was received on behalf of the eastern division of RAFA by Group-Captain J. N. D. Anderson, Chairman of the associations in the eastern region, who said that it was to be known as the H. G. Holmes Memorial Cup in memory of Mr. H. Holmes, a former member of Great Yarmouth & Gorleston RAFA, who, in his lifetime, had worked tirelessly on behalf of the Association.

Once the opening speeches were over, the audience's attention turned to the bathing beauty contest for the title of *Miss Battle of Britain* and 1961 Carnival Queen. One by one, the thirty or more contestants from as far away as Glasgow, Manchester, Birmingham and Brentford, paraded over the Marina stage in a competition judged by Dick Joice, host of Anglia TVs local news magazine programme *About Anglia*, and Drew Russell, Anglia's chief announcer. The winner was local contestant, Patricia Sewell, a 19 year old shop assistant from Anderson Road, Great Yarmouth,

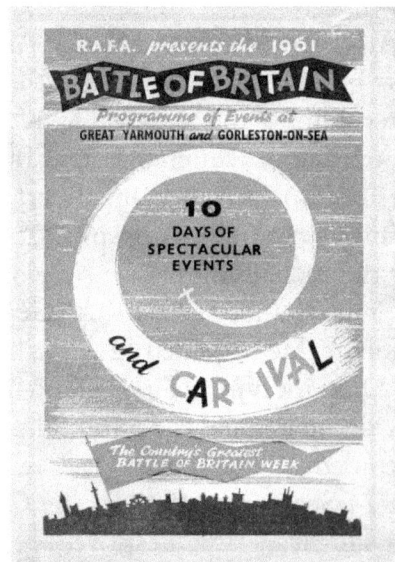

27. *The 1961 Battle of Britain commemorative programme cover.*

and the runners-up were Maria Doyle from Dublin, a dancer in the show *Paint the Town* at the Britannia Pier, and 18 year old Jackie Hunt from Kenninghall, near Diss. The winner's crown and other prizes were presented by Bruce Forsyth, star of the television programme *Saturday Night at the London Palladium* who was appearing in Bernard Delfont's summer production of *Showtime* at the Wellington Pier Pavilion.

Patricia Sewell was another of Yarmouth's highly successful bathing beauty contestants. A tall leggy blonde, Patricia learnt to dance at the Jean Boulton's school of dancing and made many concert party appearances with her dancing partner Barbara Locke. She entered her first bathing beauty contest on her 16th birthday, competing for the title of *Miss Yarmouth*, and came second. Always closely chaperoned by her mother, Patricia continued to compete in many local and national contests. She won the *Miss Battle of Britain* contest in 1959 and in the following year came second to Geraldine Bartlett. As well as winning the 1961 *Miss Battle of Britain* title, she took part in the area heats of the *Miss UK* and the *Miss England* competitions and came second in both. In 1962, Patricia went on to win the titles of *Miss Exquisite Form*, *Miss Yarmouth* and the local final of Anglia TV's *Glamour 62*, but missed the opportunity to appear in the televised contest *Holiday Town Parade* when she was disqualified for missing rehearsals.[8]

For the 1961 carnival, two parades were planned to be held on Thursday 7 September, the first in Great Yarmouth starting at 11.15am and the second in Gorleston at 3.30pm. In Great Yarmouth, the parade assembled on the Beaconsfield recreation ground, proceeded down Marine Parade to the Pleasure Beach, back along Marine Parade to Regent road, then on the Northgate Street ending on Kitchener Road. Unfortunately, the weather had taken a turn for the worse. The parade assembled in driving rain and a chill wind, and for a time, spectators were forced to shelter against convenient walls and hedges.

> At the marshalling points the rain hit some of the more fragile floats badly. Girl Guides smiled bravely as they watched the crepe paper work on their float ruined beyond repair. It was spirit like this and like that of scantily clad girls laughing as they shivered in the cold and wet that

made the morning gay. [9]

Luckily, the weather improved as the procession proceeded along Marine Parade and the sun made a temporary appearance before the rain returned with a vengeance. The weather was not the only problem confronting the procession. Even as it moved off a long-necked brontosaurus, part of a prehistoric tableau, became entangled in overhead cables and fell off its float only to be replaced unceremoniously

28. *The Watson's Motor Cup was presented each year by Watson's Garage of Great Yarmouth to the best decorated vehicle in the carnival parade.*

by a band of laughing cavemen.

> Chanting blood-curdling hunting songs, Ancient Britons recaptured the creature before it was run over by another vehicle. And after much straining and groaning the rescuers manhandled it back to its original position. [10]

Despite the weather, the carnival parade provided a grand spectacle much appreciated by the large crowds lining the route, even if they were wet. To the front of the parade was the 60-piece band of the 1st East Anglian Regiment, the Vikings, in their full ceremonial dress of blue and scarlet. The regiment, recently returned from a tour of duty in Berlin, was formed on 29 August 1959 when the Royal Norfolk and the Suffolk Regiments merged to become the 1st East Anglian Regiment. Next in line was a carriage drawn by four white horses carrying the Carnival Queen, Patricia Sewell, accompanied by the Yarmouth Amateur Operatic and Dramatic Society performer and producer, Derek Marshall, as Carnival King, and a bevy of showgirls. Following these, a model of a lifeboat on a lorry containing George Mobbs, coxswain of the Gorleston lifeboat, first mechanic Jack Bryan

29. *Great Yarmouth's commercial sector was always well-represented in the carnival parade. The numbers suggest that over 100 floats took part in this parade.*

and pupils from the Technical High School dressed in oilskins. Then came five baby elephants accompanied by jugglers, clowns, monocycle riders and other performers from the Hippodrome Circus, numerous gaily decorated floats representing many national and local firms including Andy Capp riding in the Lacon's Brewery waggon, an appropriate depiction of King Neptune with mermaids from the Yarmouth Mercury in view of the inclement weather, a gypsy caravan complete with a fortune teller, vintage cars, commercial vehicles and bands of 'red indians' and highwaymen with collecting tins. As well as the band of the Vikings, music was provided by the ceremonial band and drummers of RAF Honington, an airbase near Thetford, responsible for servicing and maintaining Britain's 'V' Bomber force, and the Administrative Apprentices Band of RAF Bircham Newton from Fakenham. Light music was provided by the Maurice Share and Gordon Edwards' dance bands while modern tastes were satisfied by rock 'n' roll music from local celebrity band Peter Jay and the Jaywalkers. As the parade made its way around town, money was collected from the forecourt of 6 Britannia Road by the Tiller girls, a high-stepping dance troupe, and a band comprised of musicians from the various summer shows.

In the evening, jazz fans were treated to the 3rd East Coast Festival of Jazz held at the Wellington Pier Winter Gardens. Publicity for the event proclaimed that the festival saw the return home of Yarmouth born Ken Colyer, a leading exponent of traditional jazz.

> At the Winter Gardens the return home of Ken Colyer and his jazzmen drew an enthusiastic crowd of about 800. The jazz fans had a five-hour feast of their favourite branch of music with two other bands – The Tom Collins jazzmen from Colchester and the Collegians jazz band with vocalist Colin Burleigh from Norwich – also taking part. The jazz festival was certainly one of the more uninhibited evenings during the week with jivers turning out in anything from ancient evening dress with wing collars, top hats and monocles to a lifelike gorilla costume.[11]

Ken Colyer's local links were at best tenuous. He was born in Great Yarmouth in 1928 when his mother was visiting relatives living in the town, but he was brought up first in London and then at Cranford in Middlesex. An interest in jazz arose while he was in the merchant navy and he quickly developed an expertise in playing the trumpet and the guitar. With a group of like-minded musicians he formed the Crane River Jazz Band in 1949. After spending some time in New Orleans, he returned to Britain in 1951 and formed the Ken Colyer Jazz Band with Lonnie Donegan on banjo, Chris Barber on trombone, Monty Sunshine on clarinet, Jim Bray on bass and Ron Bowden on drums. The release in 1953 of their LP recording entitled *New Orleans to London* is regarded by many as marking the start of the traditional jazz boom in Britain. His jazzy interpretation of American folk music, played on guitar, washboard and tea-chest bass in a trio with Lonnie Donegan and Chris Barber during the intervals at his jazz sessions is also credited with initiating the craze for the style of music called skiffle which became popular in the late 1950s.[12]

One of the more spectacular events of the week was *Skaterscades*, a roller skating variety show held at the Wellington Pier skating rink on Monday 4 September to honour Patricia Sewell, *Miss Battle of Britain*. A large audience braved the weather to watch a show of skating from the 60 amateur members of the Great Yarmouth Skating Club, orchestrated by the club's professionals Jocelyn Taylor and George Thomson. A mixture of comedy numbers, solo, double and team skating, including a dance demonstration by the club professionals who were the 1961 Professional Roller Dance Champions of Great Britain. Richard Bell was presented with the Heather Cup for the best individual free-skating performance at the Saturday evening skating competition and David Seaman was declared *Mr Roller Skating* for being the best turned out skater at the show. *Skaterscades* was immediately followed by a colourful military tattoo performed by soldiers from the 1st East Anglian Regiment.

Thunder-flashes and deafening gunfire rent the air on Monday evening at the Wellington pier Skating Rink when nearly 1700 people were transported in imagination to the jungle of Malaya by men of the 1st East Anglian Regiment, 'The Vikings', in a lifelike attack by a jungle troop on a rebel camp. The regiment were performing a brief excerpt from their celebrated Torchlight Tattoo in scenes portraying life through the ages with a definitely military flavour. Their depiction of life in ancient Yarmouth delighted the capacity crowd as did the representation of sentry duty at the time of the battle of Munden in 1759, which differed little from sentry duty today except for the picturesque uniforms.[13]

Great Yarmouth's 1961 Battle of Britain Week proved to be everything that the planners had hoped for, despite the poor weather, the money raised amounted to an impressive £1,832, of which £235 was donated towards maintaining the RNLI Gorleston Lifeboat, exceeding the previous year's record total. In recognition of this achievement, Air

Vice-Marshall Sir Geoffrey Bromet presented the Battle of Britain Trophy for the second year running to Mr. R. G. Moore, Chairman of the Yarmouth & Gorleston RAFA at the opening ceremony of the 1962 festival week that was also held at the Marina.

By the late 1960s and early 1970s, cheap continental holidays and a run of years with poor summer weather were reducing the number of visitors to Great Yarmouth, especially at the September end of the season. By 1971, the takings from Battle of Britain Week had reduced from an average of £1,800 to a mere £500 and, as a result, Great Yarmouth & Gorleston RAFA decided to abandon the festival and concentrate their efforts simply on the Wings Day street collection. In the words of the RAFA vice-chairman, there were "*too few to remember 'The Few'. Shortening memories, a shortage of helpers and a shortage of money in the public's pockets are slowly killing Yarmouth's Battle of Britain Week*".[14] In 1971, the festival week was replaced by a *Ride with the Stars* charity day and a procession along the seafront promenade organised by the management of Botton Brother's Pleasure Beach, when stars from the various summer shows gave their time to sell autographs, lucky number programmes and join the processional ride along Regent

1   Flight Magazine, 29 August 1946.
2   Yarmouth Mercury, 7 July 1923.
3   *Ibid.*, 14 September 1951.
4   *Ibid.*, 15 September 1950.
5   *Ibid.*, 23 September 1955.
6   *Ibid.*, 24 September 1971.
7   For biographical details of Harold Bird-Wilson see a) *Daily Telegraph*, obituary, 29 December 2000; b) www.rafweb.org/biographies/Bird-Wilson; c) www.raf. mod.uk/bbmf, Hurricane P3878 and 'Birdy' Bird-Wilson by Clive Rowley
8   *Ibid. 2*, 18 September 1959; Eastern Daily Press, Friday 1 September 1961; *Ibid.*, 8 September 1961.
9   *Ibid.*, 8 September 1961.
10   Eastern Daily Press, Friday 8 September 1961.
11   *Ibid. 2*, 15 Sept 1961.
12   For details of Ken Colyer's life and music see the Colyer website at www. kencolyer.org.
13   *Ibid. 2*, 8 September 1961.
14   *Ibid.*, 24 September 1971.

Road and the Marine Parade.

Great Yarmouth's Annual Battle of Britain Week, 1961
Programme of Events

Thursday 31 August.
3.00pm, *Grand Opening* of the *Battle of Britain Week* followed by the *Miss Battle of Britain & 1961 Carnival Queen* Bathing Beauty Contest and a performance of the show *Blow Your Top* at the Marina.
8.00–11.30pm, *Jazz at the Winter Garden* featuring The Clyde Valley Stompers and Tucker Smith's Anglian Jazz Band, and including a cabaret by the Cherry B TV Twins.
Friday 1 September.
7.00pm, *Children's Talent Competition* at the Marina.
7.30pm, a *Grand Bingo Drive* at the Conservative Club, Theatre Plain, organised by the Great Yarmouth British Legion.
Saturday 2 September.
1.00–5.00pm, a *Grand Roller Skating Festival* at the Wellington Pier skating rink, including the *National Free Skating Competition* for the Heather Cup (presented by G.J. Holmes) and *Mr and Miss Roller Skating Competition* (prizes sponsored by Nestlé).
3.15pm, *The Grand Battle of Britain Swimming Gala* held at the Great Yarmouth Bathing Pool featuring a triangular competition for the Battle of Britain Cup (donated by C.P. Palmer), involving races and water polo matches, between the Great Yarmouth, Norwich Swan and Ipswich Swimming Clubs.
Sunday 3 September.
An all-day 18-hole *Open Golf Tournament* held at the Great Yarmouth & Caister Golf Club (prizes by T.A. Watson, Club Captain).
Monday 4 September.
7.30pm, a Carnival performance of *Skaterscades* roller skating show at the Wellington Pier skating rink, featuring the resident professionals, Jocelyn Taylor and George Thompson, and 60 members of the Great Yarmouth Roller Skating club followed by an evening *Victory Torchlight Tattoo* presented by the 1st East Anglian Regiment.
7.30pm, a *Progressive Whist Drive* at the Conservative Club, Theatre Square.
Tuesday 5 September; Kiddies Day.
10.00am, *Children's Beach Sports Day* on the Central Beach behind the

Marina.

2.30pm, a *Sand Modelling Competition* on Gorleston Beach behind the Floral Hall.

Wednesday 6 September; Teenagers Day.

3.00pm, *Carnival Capers* at the Wellington Pier Winter Gardens.

Thursday 7 September.

A *Grand Carnival Procession* at 11.15am through Great Yarmouth and 3.30pm in Gorleston; proceeds to be shared between the R.A.F.A Benevolent Fund and the Gorleston Lifeboat. The Watson Motor Cup to be awarded to the best decorated vehicle (presented by Watson's Garage Ltd).

8.00pm, the annual *Carnival Night Dance* at Waveney Farm, St Olaves.

8.00pm, *The 3rd East Coast Festival of Jazz* at the Wellington Pier Winter Gardens featuring the Great Yarmouth-born jazz musician, Ken Colyer, the Collegians and other East Anglian Traditional Jazz bands with a £5 prize for the best fancy dress.

Friday 8 September.

3.00pm, a *Children's Fancy Dress Competition* at the Marina.

8.00pm, *The Battle of Britain Carnival Ball* at the Wellington Pier Winter Gardens, at which Tommy Steele and his wife are to present competition prizes.

Saturday 9 September.

2.00pm, *Carnival Time* at the Wellington Pier skating rink, including a competition between Great Yarmouth and London for the Battle of Britain Trophy.

A *Crack the Safe Competition* on the Marina car-park to find the combination of a Remington 'Safetifile' to win the prizes contained inside (prizes sponsored by Remington Rand Ltd – Shaver Division).

Saturday 16 September.

Wings Day street collection.

Sunday 17 September.

A *Sea Angling Competition* along the beach at the Gorleston Bend for the RAFA Challenge Cup, The Linda Cup and the Ann Baker Memorial Cup.

11.00am, *Thanksgiving Service* at St Nicholas Parish Church.

Ongoing Events during Battle of Britain Week

A *Monster Balloon Race* (the winner of the balloon that travels the furthest to receive a £50 premium bond sponsored by Nestlé), the famous *OSKY*

Straw game and *Cover a Spitfire in Pennies,* all from the Marina Car Park, manned and organised by the Osky family from Birmingham.

A *Best Decorated House or Shop Window* competition; the winner to be presented with £10 and the Carnival Premises Cup (donated by Mrs. D Larwood).

'Guess the Weight' Carnival Cake Competition organised by Matthes Bakery and Restaurant on Kings Street – the winner takes the cake.

The *Carnival Sweet Competition* – guess the number of sweets in a jar - organised by Asplen's Sweet Shop, Regent Road (prizes donated by Mr. S.C. Asplen).

A *Beautiful Baby Competition* (held on Thursday 24 August at St Johns Church Hall, Lancaster Road) organised by the Battle of Britain Committee for the Battle of Britain Silver Challenge Cup.

A *Waiter's Race*, competing for the Lacon's Trophy (donated by Lacon's Brewery Ltd) and organised by the Great Yarmouth Lions Club.

Daily flying displays of aircraft from RAF Coltishall and Air-Sea Rescue demonstrations in conjunction with the RNLI.

An Air-Sea Rescue launch located on the Hall Quay Open for view every day during Battle of Britain Week,.

A *Scramble* exhibition in the Exhibition Hall at the New Central Library illustrating all aspects of life in the RAF.

Battle of Britain Photographic Competition for black & white and colour photographs on any theme related to an event in Battle of Britain Week. Closing date September 30, winner of each class receives a Kodak camera.

Miss Battle of Britain winners

Year.	Miss Battle of Britain	Venue	Crowned by
1946	*Hazel Gay*	Marina	Norman Pett
1947	*Patricia Hall*	Wellington Pier	
1948	*Sylvia Newsom*	Britannia Pier	
1949	*Margaret Leggett*	Windmill	
1950	*Sylvia King*	Windmill	
1951	*Joyce Kempster*	Windmill	
1952	*Joan Hibbott*	Windmill	
1953	*Maureen Pitchers*	Marina	Len Howe

1954	*Maureen Pitchers*	Marina	
1955	*Marianne Hatton*	Marina	Vera Lynn
1956	*Sheila Lewis*	Marina	Yana
1957	*Toni Pendyck*	Marina	Norman Wisdom
1958	*Doreen Dixon*	Marina	Alma Cogan
1959	*Patricia Sewell*	Marina	Ken Dodd
1960	*Geraldine Bartlett*	Marina	Charlie Drake
1961	*Patricia Sewell*	Marina	Bruce Forsyth
1962	*Mary Taylor*	Marina	Harry Secombe
1963	*Nina Mott*	Marina	Ken Dodd
1964	*Mary Taylor*	Marina	Morecambe & Wise
1965	*Pauline Thorpe*	Marina	The Batchelors
1966	*June Philpot*	Marina	Frank Ifield
1967	*Margaret Yardy*	Marina	Rolf Harris
1968	*Marie Fisher*	Marina	Jimmy Tarbuck
1969	*Carolyn Grey*	Marina	Jack Douglas
1970	*Carolyn Grey*	Marina	Sid James

6

Miss Yarmouth and Other Competitions

The tradition of choosing a young, single woman to become queen for the day at a local festival or carnival was far from new. May Queens were a common feature of traditional May Day celebrations in many rural communities and a Harvest Queen often led a procession during a village summer carnival. As it was normally the most attractive and intelligent young woman that was chosen, her selection might well be considered an early form of beauty contest. In the early 1900s most towns and cities, like Great Yarmouth, had designated Hospital Days during which various activities were held to raise funds for their local hospitals. Most fund-raising days included a carnival procession and, usually, leading the parade was a carnival queen, sometimes accompanied by the carnival king. Often the carnival king was portrayed as an older comical character but his queen was normally a young woman in her prime. Sometimes both were chosen by the carnival's organising committee but at other times the choice was by a ballot or a beauty contest.

All of the carnival weeks that were held at Great Yarmouth in 1922, 1923 and 1934, as well as the Jubilee celebrations of 1935, involved carnival kings and queens. Ailsa Woodger was elected by the Great

30. Rose Addy, Miss Yarmouth 1934. This illustration was taken from the Official 1934 Grand Carnival Souvenir Programme printed for the Great Yarmouth Corporation by Jarrold & Sons of Norwich.

Yarmouth Carnival Committee to be the carnival queen for the duration of the pageant held in July 1934. In the 1930s, attractive young women were often chosen to represent and publicise a product, a factory, an industry or a town, especially a holiday town like Great Yarmouth. Mostly they were selected because of their personality, intelligence and facial beauty, and represented their industry or town in other beauty or personality competitions and appeared at promotional functions and events on behalf of their sponsors. At a Carnival Ball held in the Wellington Pier Pavilion on 8 June 1934, Miss Rose Addy was chosen by a public ballot to be *Miss Yarmouth*, not only to represent the borough during the July carnival week and at functions throughout the coming year, but also to assist Miss Woodger during the hospital carnival procession in August. Amongst her civic duties on behalf of the Town Council, Miss Addy acted as host to Emmie Plant, *Miss Macclesfield Silk Queen*, during her visit to Great Yarmouth during Privilege Week of 1935. The week 22 to 29 June 1935 was designated by the Town Council as a Privilege Week, an experiment in which visitors from a selected industrial town were given certain privileges in an attempt to attract early summer season holidaymakers, including financial assistance with their transport costs; a generous inducement at a time when few blue-collar workers received holidays with pay. Representatives from that town were also invited by the Town Council to visit and inspect the facilities of Great Yarmouth in an attempt to promote the resort as a holiday destination for its factory workers. In 1935, the targeted town was Macclesfield.

In a similar attempt to improve the historic link with Leicester and promote Great Yarmouth as the preferred seaside destination

GREAT YARMOUTH AND GORLESTON-ON-SEA.

SPECIAL PRIVILEGE PERIODS TO VISITORS

June 19th to July 3rd, 1937 (inclusive)

and

September 11th to 18th, 1937 (inclusive).

On application to the Borough Treasurer, Town Hall, Great Yarmouth, enclosing 3/- (for one week) or 6/- (for two weeks) (children under 14 years of age half price) special facilities will be offered to all bona fide visitors to the Borough, staying during the above periods.

The **WEEKLY** privilege tickets will be available as follows:

1st Week—from June 19th to 26th.

2nd Week—from June 26th to July 3rd.

3rd Week—from September 11th to 18th.

entitling the owner, without further charge, to the use of the Corporation's Bowling Greens, Tennis Courts (including **(Cumberland Turf Greens excepted)** Sundays), Waterways and Pleasure Boats, Boating Lakes and Yacht Ponds, and admission to the Bathing Pool (to view or bathe) and the Wellington Pier.

In addition to the above, the following further facilities will be granted:—

On presentation of the Privilege Ticket, reduced fares will be charged by the Great Yarmouth and Gorleston Steamboat Co., Ltd., on their steamer trips to the Norfolk Broads, etc., and books of concession tickets available for various amusements at the Pleasure Beach will be issued at a reduced charge upon application at the Kiosk at the entrance, also reduced prices will be granted to the Wellington Pier Pavilion and Winter Gardens Ballroom.

Any further particulars will be gladly furnished on application to the Publicity Manager (G.W.), Great Yarmouth.

31. Privilege Weeks were introduced by the Town Council as an inducement to factory workers from the Midlands to choose Great Yarmouth as their holiday destination.

for Leicester's factory workers, the Publicity Committee invited *Miss Leicester*, Vivian Yesson-Richards, and her five attendants to visit Great Yarmouth from 5 July until 12 July 1937 to inspect Yarmouth's many holiday attractions, accompanied throughout on this occasion by Jean Davey, *Miss Yarmouth* 1937.   During his welcoming address to *Miss Leicester* at an official reception held in her honour at the Town Hall, the Mayor stated that the people and Town Council of Great Yarmouth had:

> for many years been connected with Leicester and they had welcomed many thousands of Leicester people to the town. They appreciated the fact that the Leicester people patronised Yarmouth in such very great numbers. He was certain these people would appreciate the great improvements they had made – particularly the Marina, which was now the beauty spot of the Front and had taken the place of a rather dirty sandy patch.[1]

While in all these cases the young women were considered to be beauty queens, it was their facial beauty and personality that won them their titles. Not one of them was selected as a result of a bathing beauty competition.

However by the mid-1930s the growing fashion for suntans among many young people and the discovery of swimming as a cheap recreational activity accessible to all, gave an impetus to the development of more fashionable swimwear. The ugly wool and jersey cover-all swimsuits of the 1920s gradually gave way to more revealing backless cotton based costumes for women with lower necklines and higher cut legs, often with small overskirts designed to hide the thighs and provide an element of modesty while sunbathing on the beach. Once medical opinion had given its support to the health giving effects of sunlight on the body, sunbathing promoted an interest in the beauty of the whole woman and not just the face. In an attempt to involve the Town Council more actively in Great Yarmouth's Hospital Day, the Hospital Procession Committee invited the Council, through its Beach & Promenade Committee, to organise a competition to select the 1939 carnival queen. As a result a bathing beauty competition was proposed and subsequently held at the Marina, in which the contestants paraded before the competition judges dressed in bathing costumes. The event consisted of two preliminary rounds held during evening dances at the Marina on consecutive Fridays, 14 and 21 July, and a Grand Final on Friday 28 July. The eventual winner, 21 year old brunette Freda Belcher, a holidaymaker from Manchester, was chosen by audience applause to be *Miss Yarmouth* 1939 and the town's carnival queen for Hospital Day on 10 August.

Bathing beauty competitions involving young women dressed in swimsuits was an idea that had developed in America and was only adopted by most British seaside holiday-resorts after World War Two. The first major US inter-city bathing beauty contest was held at the American seaside holiday resort of Atlantic City, New Jersey in 1921. The contest was conceived by H. Conrad Eckholm of the Atlantic City Businessmen's League as a means of attracting tourists to the resort at the quiet end of the summer holiday season, and was held each year during Atlantic City's September Fall Frolic. The first winner, recipient of the Golden Mermaid Trophy and prize-money of 100 dollars, was 16 year old Margaret Gorman from Washington DC who was subsequently described as being *Miss America* by a local newspaper, a title that was adopted by the contest organisers and awarded to every subsequent winner. The competition was abandoned for a short period from 1929 to 1932, partly as a result of the American Stock Market crash and partly due to public criticism regarding the nature of the contest – too much naked flesh on show for the more conservative among the members of the American public – as well as for the inappropriate behaviour of some of the contestants. The contest was restored in 1933 and renamed the *Miss America Pageant*, with an emphasis on talent and intellectual skill as well as physical beauty, and quickly gained in popularity throughout the USA.[2] During World War Two, many of the *Miss America* beauty queens achieved public respect by advertising war bonds and entertaining troops at home and overseas. Their photographs and portraits adorned many barrack room walls, the noses of allied bombers and were taken to war in the pockets of servicemen in both the US and British armed forces. One *Miss America* contestant, Dorothy Lamour, became famous as a film star frequently

32. Neville Bishop takes charge during a heat of the 1948 Miss Yarmouth competition. (AR)

appearing on the cinema screen dressed in a sarong.

Undoubtedly, contact between the American and British forces helped to encourage the demand for similar bathing beauty competitions in peacetime Britain. The first official post-war British bathing beauty contest was allegedly held at Morecambe in August 1945. Entitled the *Bathing Beauty Queen Contest*, the competition was organised by the local town council and sponsored by the Sunday Dispatch newspaper. The winner received a trophy, seven guineas and a basket of fruit. Nevertheless, the event became an annual summertime attraction and thrived to become the nationally famous *Miss Great Britain* contest. By the 1960s, the prize money awarded to the winner exceeded £1000.[3]

While beauty competitions were common in Britain during the 1930s, bathing beauty contests were not accepted so readily by the more conservative middle class members of the public. Therefore, the decision by the Great Yarmouth Town Council to select the carnival queen of 1939 by a bathing beauty competition was indeed a bold move, and one that clearly reflected a desire to develop popular entertainments that would appeal to the growing number of working-class holidaymakers who were visiting the resort in the late 1930s. Most contemporary histories of seaside beauty competitions claim that the 1945 *Bathing Beauty Queen Contest* held at Morecambe was not only the first council sponsored post-war competition but also the first bathing beauty competition ever to be held in Great Britain. It is an indisputable fact that the Great Yarmouth Town Council's decision to hold a bathing beauty contest in 1939 preceded Morecambe's by six years and it was only the outbreak of World War Two in the following September that has obscured Great Yarmouth's genuine claim to fame.

The Marina's tradition of holding annual bathing beauty competitions began even earlier, and with the Great Yarmouth Town Council's clear encouragement and approval. In 1937, the Town Council advertised in the local Great Yarmouth Mercury for *"Beautiful girls to compete for Best Figure and Smartest Bathing Costume"*[4] in a contest to be held at the newly opened Marina. As a result, 200 girls responded and took part in a bathing beauty competition that was sponsored by the national Daily Mirror newspaper and compered by the Marina's resident comedian, Billy Matchett. The winner was Jean Davey, a slim, blonde 14 year old high school girl from Southtown Road, Great Yarmouth[5], who received the modest prize of a dressing case, which was presented to her by Mrs. P. Ellis, wife of Alderman Ellis, the Chairman of Great Yarmouth Town Council's Beach Committee. In the same year, the Town Council even suggested holding a Scottish beauty queen contest during the herring fishing season.

At a meeting held in March 1947, Councillor Chittleburgh, Chairman of Great Yarmouth's Entertainments and Publicity Committee proposed that a bathing beauty competition should be held at the council-owned Marina every week during the summer months for the title of *Miss Yarmouth*, and that £200 of the committee's budget should be allocated for prize money and other expenses. The first post-war *Miss Yarmouth* competition, a personality competition for dancers in conventional dress, was held in 1946 at a dance in the Goodes Hotel where Miss Margaret Evans was chosen as the winner by audience applause. As a result of Councillor Chittlebugh's proposal, from 1947 *Miss Yarmouth* was elected by a bathing beauty competition. The 1947 competition was held every Wednesday for 18 weeks during the summer season and the winners of each week's heat were invited to take part in a grand final on Wednesday 3 September 1947 at the Marina. Judged by celebrities Leslie Mitchell and Dulcie Gray, and the boxer Bruce Woodcock, the final was won by a local woman, Mary Spinks, a young hospital

33. Frankie Howard seems in a daze as he presents Audrey Harding from Oxford, a second-time competition winner, with her 1950 Miss Yarmouth sash. (Archant)

receptionist from Shrublands in Gorleston. Initially individual prizes were small, with the 18 winners of the weekly competition heats held during the 1947 summer season receiving a mere £3 in prize money, but as the competition gained in popularity the prizes improved so that the winner of the 1950 *Miss Yarmouth* competition, Audrey Harding from Oxford, received a remuneration of £50 and a box of bloaters, presented to her by the comedian Frankie Howard.

> Twenty-one year old Mrs Audrey Harding of Oxford, selected as *Miss Yarmouth* last year, retained her title yesterday when an audience of over 3000 at the Marina saw Frankie Howard, the BBC *Variety Bandbox* comedian, drape the silk sash of office over her shoulder, re-enacting a ceremony performed a year ago by film actress Joan Hopkins.[6]

During the early years of the competition many of the contestants were local women and the most successful of these was Mary Spinks. Mary Elizabeth Spinks was born in Great Yarmouth on 27 December 1933, daughter of G. H. Spinks, Yarmouth's Chief Sanitary Inspector, and won her first *Miss Yarmouth* crown at the tender age of fourteen. Mary continued to compete for the title every year and was successful for the second time in 1951, although even then her age was incorrectly reported.

> *Miss Yarmouth* 1947 wins again. Miss Mary Spinks, a 21 year old shorthand typist of 19a, St Catherine's Way, Magdalen College Estate, Gorleston on Thursday became the second girl since the war to be twice elected *Miss Yarmouth*. Mrs Audrey Harding of Oxford, who held the title for the past two years, did not seek to complete the hat-trick but a letter of good wishes from her was read from the stage of the Marina by Mr Will Browning, the manager, who had been responsible for running the contest throughout the summer. Miss Spinks was *Miss Yarmouth* 1947, and had been in the first three in each contest since then. Two years ago she won the title of Miss Lowestoft.[7]

Mary was a talented dancer and actress, and without doubt her appearances in numerous bathing beauty competitions helped to advance her career on the stage. In her early years, she trained at the Phyllis Adams School of Dancing as a speciality dancer and eventually joined the ranks of the Yarmouth Amateur Operatic and Dramatic Society where she displayed her acting talents through leading parts in various musical and dramatic productions during the early 1950s. A professional career in acting under the stage name of Mary Miller began in 1959 with an appearance in a television production of *The Golden Spur*. In 1963, she became one of the founding members of the National Theatre Company under the artistic direction of Laurence Olivier. A long and successful career in acting included an appearance in the TV drama *Dr Finlay's Casebook* where she met and subsequently married the Scottish actor William Simpson at Port Monteith, Stirlingshire on 24 July 1965.[8] Her most celebrated role was as the barrister Angela Dunwoody QC in the court room drama series, *Crown Court*.

Mary's five years as a successful bathing beauty contestant is testament to her exceptional physical beauty. However, the absence of any mention of her participation in bathing beauty competitions in her many biographies shows clearly that they were considered not to be accepted behaviour in polite society and that the intelligence and morality of the participants was frequently called into question by sensation-seeking newspapers and some sections of the general public.

In the early 1950s, bathing beauty competitions were not to everybody's taste and, in 1952, the Town Council responded to prevailing public opinion by abandoning the *Miss Yarmouth* contest and replacing it at the Marina with a weekly *Miss Holiday Girl* competition where contestants were judged on their personality, daintiness and deportment, and were required to wear any clothes of their choice other than bathing costumes. The Chairman of the Town Council's Entertainments & Publicity Committee justified this change by stating that the public had become tired of bathing beauty competitions and wanted a contest that anyone could win and a competition that nobody was allowed to compete in more than once. Covering one such contest, a Yarmouth Mercury reporter commented that:

> Elderly charm won the day over youth in a competition
> in which charm and personality in addition to deportment
> and general appearance are taken into consideration by the
> judges.[9]

The *Miss Holiday Girl* contest ran for a further two years until 1955 when the *Miss Yarmouth* competition was reinstated due to popular demand and a general easing in public opinion regarding the nature and suitability of these contests. An alternative charm contest had also been held at the Marina between 1950 and 1956 under the title of the *Miss Personality Girl* competition, a contest to discover the competitor whose head most resembled that of the girl who appeared on the advertising poster for the makers of Personality Turtle Oil Soap. That too succumbed to the growing demand for bathing beauty contests, encouraged by the increasing popularity nationwide of Eric Morley's *Miss World* competitions.

By the late 1950s, bathing beauty contests were an essential element in any seaside resort's holiday entertainment and in Great Yarmouth the Marina was the natural place for such competitions to be held.

As well as the *Miss Battle of Britain* and *Miss Yarmouth* competitions the Marina hosted many other beauty contests including *Miss Poppet Girl* and *Miss Exquisite Form*, and, from 1957, the Sunday Pictorial sponsored a 'Marilyn Monroe' Beach Beauty contest on the sands behind the Marina. From 1955, the newly reinstated bathing beauty competition for the title of *Miss Yarmouth* once again consisted of weekly heats at the Marina with the winners of each heat competing in a grand final during late August or early September. The winner of the *Miss Yarmouth* 1955 competition was Norma Wilson who was presented with her crown by Tommy Trinder on 9 September during the Yarmouth Old Folks' Rally at the Marina.

34. Local contestant Carolyn Grey, Miss Great Yarmouth 1971. (Archant)

In 1959, the BBC began televising the *Miss World* competition and, not to be outdone, in 1961 Anglia Television included a beauty contest in its variety programme *Showdate* that was televised live from Great Yarmouth's Britannia Pier theatre. The following year Anglia TV began the first of its annual summer season *Glamour* competitions, a bathing beauty contest in which the preliminary heats were televised in turn every week during the summer season from one of the many holiday towns in the Anglia region. In order to continue the tradition of a *Miss Yarmouth*, the winner of the Great Yarmouth heat of this annual competition was henceforth awarded with the honorary title of *Miss Yarmouth*. The 1962 Great Yarmouth heat, held at the Garibaldi Hotel, was won by a local contestant, Patricia Sewell from Alderson Road, who had previously won the title of *Miss Battle of Britain* in both 1959 and 1961. At the end of the season, the winners of all the weekly contests competed for the title of *Miss Anglia Region* in a grand televised final, the first of which was also held at the Britannia Pier in Great Yarmouth. That too was won by Patricia Sewell who, as *Miss Anglia*, went on to represent the region in an all-England contest.

The *Glamour* programmes became extremely popular with the viewing public and continued to be an important part of Anglia's summer schedule for the next 25 years. With the retirement of Neville Bishop at the end of the 1959 summer season, the nature of the entertainment at the Marina gradually changed and after 1960 bathing beauty contests were no longer a major feature. Television needed the security of an indoor venue for the live broadcasts, such as the Garibaldi Hotel or the Britannia Pier Theatre, and the weather-affected Marina was not considered a suitable place to hold the Great Yarmouth heats. Nevertheless, for a few seasons the preliminary selection of the six or more competitors who were to appear in the evening live televised heat was made during an afternoon contest at the Marina.

In what might be seen as a futile effort to rekindle a waning interest in the Marina as a place of entertainment, in 1970 the Town Council reintroduced its own *Miss Yarmouth* bathing beauty competition at the venue, sponsored by John Player and Company, the cigarette manufacturers, with a first prize to the winner of £250 and an automatic place in the national *Miss England* competition. During the year following her crowning, the winner was expected to travel throughout the country attending functions and events publicising Great Yarmouth as a holiday town. This competition continued at the Marina until that venue finally closed, when it was transferred to the council owned Wellington Pier and renamed as the *Miss British Isles* contest. The 1976 title of *Miss British Isles* was won by Colchester born Gillian Clarke who became better known as a member of the popular dance troupe, Legs & Co.

---

1   Yarmouth Mercury, 10 July 1937.
2   For information relating to the Miss America contest see various internet sites, particularly "Beauty Pageants" in www.buzzle.com.
3   For information relating to UK contests see "A Brief History: The Rise and Decline of Seaside Beauty Contests" in www.mac.ndo.co.uk.
4   *Ibid. 1*, 22 July 1937.

5   *Ibid.*, 26 August 1937.
6   Eastern Evening News, 1 September 1950.
7   *Ibid. 1*, 7 September 1951.
8   *Ibid.*, 30 July 1965.
9   *Ibid.*, 18 July 1952.

Miss Great Yarmouth Bathing Beauty Queens

Year.	Miss Great Yarmouth	Venue
1946	*Margaret Evans*	Goodes
1947	*Mary Spinks*	Marina
1948	*Patricia Brown*	Marina
1949	*Audrey Harding*	Marina
1950	*Audrey Harding*	Marina
1951	*Mary Spinks*	Marina
1955	*Norma Wilson*	Marina
1956	*Margaret Saunders*	Marina
1957	*Mary Williams*	Marina
1958	*Margaret England*	Marina
1959	*Jacqueline Peterson*	Marina
1960	*Mary de Mor & Jean Meyering (2 winners)*	Marina
1961	*Anita Johnsson*	Marina
1962	*Patricia Sewell*	Garibaldi
1970	*Kathleen O'Neil*	Marina
1971	*Carolyn Grey*	Marina
1972	*Wendy Ann George*	Marina
1973	*Christine Owen*	Marina

35. *A crowded Marine Parade of 1960 from a Mason's Alpha Series postcard produced for Walker and Wilson's, newsagents, of Darlington. Great Yarmouth was a holiday destination for many of Darlington's industrial workers.*

7

A White Elephant on The Promenade

The late nineteen fifties were not only the high point in Great Yarmouth's popularity as a seaside resort but also of the Marina as the foremost place of entertainment on the promenade. Neville Bishop was without doubt a hard act to follow. His retirement marked the beginning of a downward change in the fortunes of the Marina. Where Great Yarmouth was concerned, the closure of the Peterborough to Great Yarmouth section of the Midland and Great Northern Railway in 1959, together with the Beeching line closures of 1963 isolated the resort from its main holiday catchment area in the Midlands. Birmingham and Leicester no longer had a direct rail connection with the town. Holidaymakers from the industrial midland counties were now subject to long and tiring journeys by car or coach to their holiday destination along an inadequate road network, often ending in long queues of vehicles on the approaches to the town. Most Saturday mornings during the summer season, traffic into and out of Great Yarmouth was slow and often at a standstill. The port facilities were also in decline and the herring industry was collapsing due to over-fishing mainly by fishing boats from the Continent. If this were not enough, competition from cheap package holidays to the Continent

36. *Mr Give-away, Bob Andrews, and the cast of the 1960 production Strike it Lucky.*

and elsewhere was starting to take its toll. Mass advertising in the press and on television was having an effect. The allure of the guaranteed sunshine and warm seas of a Mediterranean resort was more attractive to many than a stay in an often windy and wet Norfolk seaside town.

Therefore it was important that Neville Bishop was replaced at the Marina by an attractive up-to-date entertainment that would appeal to all ages. The director of the Entertainment and Publicity Committee

> … recommended that Show Band type of entertainment be discontinued; to be replaced by entertainment of a light concert party type with a slight increase in the prices of admission for adults but retaining the existing admission charge for children at 1/-.[1]

Richard Stone Productions Limited was given the task of putting together a variety show that would appeal to the holiday visitor. The result was a twice daily two hour show called *Strike it Lucky* performed in a format that was popular at that time with television audiences and where members of the public were encouraged to come on stage and compete in games for prizes; an entertainment in the manner of Michael Miles' *Take Your Pick* and Hughie Green's *Double Your Money*.

Performances ran from 4 June 1960 for 16 weeks. The compere for the show was Bob Andrews, better known as Mr Give-away, who was assisted by a shapely hostess, Laura Thurlow. Prizes included popular Dansette record players, electric blankets and automatic teasmades.

In between competitions and games, music was provided by the Eddie Mendoza Quartet with Stanley King at the organ together with performances from a number of variety artists including a crazy musical act from Roy Earl, acrobatics from the Five Robertis, Dill Russell an escapologist, songs from the soprano Joanne Michelle and slapstick humour from the Entrebors, a group of Swedish clowns. Eddie Mendoza was a good substitute for Neville Bishop. Comedian and accordionist Mendoza was born in 1913 at Aberdeen and became infamous on stage for his off-beat humour and large droopy eight-inch handlebar moustache. He toured with the well-known comedy duo Flanagan and Allen for ENSA during World War Two and afterwards formed his own band, The Archer Street Spivs, who became renowned for their lively music and manic comedy. As an additional attraction, the Finance and Law Committee had also approved a grant of £700 for the purchase of an Austin A40 motor car to be used as a prize in a competition to guess the total number of admissions to the Marina during the 16 weeks of the summer season. The competition was won by a Mr. Arthur Scott of Towcester who had estimated the number of admissions to be 107,934, only 74 more than the actual figure of 107,860. The car was subsequently presented to him by the Mayor, Mr W.E. Mobbs at a special event held at the Marina on 3 October 1960.[2]

Although *Strike it Lucky* proved to be a very successful summer show, a repeat of the same for the 1961 season was not possible because Eddie Mendoza had moved abroad to live in Australia. Instead Great Yarmouth-based Maurice Share and his Starnotes Orchestra headed a variety show called *Blow Your Top*, playing up-tempo music and performing comedy turns supported by singer Pauline Goodman, comedian and compere Barry Crane and Reg Taylor and Sanga, a mental telepathy act. Talent competitions gave members of the Marina's audience chances to win big prizes. Comedian Sandy Sandford, star of Anglia Television's *Afternoon Club* and *The Junior Angle Club*, was

37. Wrestling was a popular attraction in 1963. As audiences dwindled, Wednesday evening variety shows at the Marina gave way to better attended wrestling tournaments organised by Dale Martin Promotions Ltd. (Archant)

recruited to present a daily children's party each morning with games, competitions and a junior talent contest.

Every Wednesday the central area of the Marina was cleared to allow for evening bouts of wrestling in an attempt to vary the entertainment available at the venue. Wrestling matches had become a feature of Saturday afternoon viewing on ITV since they were first broadcast from the West Ham Baths on 9 November 1955. By 1961, televised wrestling competitions, introduced by an enthusiastic Kent Walton, had made household names of wrestlers such as Jackie Pallo, Billy Two Rivers, Mick McManus, Joe Cornelius and Shirley Crabtree, the Blonde Adonis, soon to be known as Big Daddy. Viewers of all ages and from all levels in society quickly acquired a taste for the sport. Even the Queen and the Duke of Edinburgh were reported to be avid Saturday afternoon viewers. To capitalise on its popularity, the Entertainments and Publicity Committee had agreed to the request from Dale Martin

Promotions Limited for the use of the Marina to host wrestling tournaments for at least one evening a week during the summer season.[3] Despite the unpredictable British weather, well attended open-air wrestling tournaments were held there every Wednesday from 1961 until 1973 and in some years on Mondays and Saturdays as well.

Variety was the theme for the 1962 summer season in a vain attempt to arrest falling audience numbers. A different show every day with different performers in each was the aim, in the hope of attracting repeat visits from individual holidaymakers.

38. *This advert clearly illustrates that by 1970 wrestling had become the main attraction at the Marina.*

To comply with the limitations still in place on the nature of Sunday entertainments, Sunday afternoons at the Marina were devoted mainly to brass band concerts under the title *Summer Serenade* and regularly featured local bands. The 1961 season began on Whit Sunday, 3 June with a grand brass band concert given by the Snibston Colliery Miner's Welfare Band from Leicestershire. Throughout the season bands from Kings Lynn, Cambridge, Haverhill, Newmarket, Long Melford, Dereham and the Norwich Lads Club featured during the Sunday concerts at the Marina.

Bruce 'Bunny' Barron, an impresario from Broadstairs, well-known for producing summer seaside variety shows and Christmastime pantomimes, was given the task of putting together shows for the Monday, Tuesday and Friday evenings. Under the banner 'Bunny Barron Presents', the Monday attraction was *The Leslie Adams Show*, on Tuesday it was *The Sunshine Follies* and on Friday, a give-away show with the title *Something for Nothing*. Demonstrations of the latest dance craze, the twist, from Milton Ingram and the Dynamic Continental Twisters followed by a twist contest for the general public added a modern contemporary element to each of the shows. Heats of the twist competition were held during the Monday and Tuesday shows and the top performers in these competed again in a grand final on the Friday, all to music from a little known rock 'n' roll band, Norman Jago and the Jaguars.

Every Thursday afternoon and evening, local entertainers Sandy Sandford and Maurice Share, with his Starnotes Orchestra, headlined a variety show entitled *You're the Tops*. In the afternoon show Sandy Sandford compered the hotly contested *You're the Tops* Bathing Beauty Competition and in the evening the *You're the Tops* Amateur Talent Show. Wednesdays and Saturdays were devoted to wrestling tournaments. Every morning Sandy Sandford played the genial host of *The TV Comics Show*, a party for children.

The same format was adopted for the 1963 summer season with a different show every afternoon and evening. The George Slater Orchestra provided the music, replacing Maurice Share as the resident orchestra, and a *Crackerjack* theme permeated throughout drawing on ideas from the children's TV show of the same name. Despite the variety on offer, audiences were gradually declining. Without the funds necessary to draw in big star names the quality of performances was often inferior to that of the variety shows elsewhere in Great Yarmouth as well as on television. Many holidaymakers preferred to watch programmes on the television sets that were making an appearance in the lounges of their holiday accommodation than sit through a chilly evening's show at the Marina. At the end of the season Sandy Sandford retired as host at the Marina to become the full-time

39. *Programme cover for Swing Along, featuring the Eddie Hemmings' All Star Orchestra.*

resident entertainer at the newly
established Vauxhall Holiday Park on
the outskirts of the town.

The 1964 summer season saw a
return to the format made popular
by Neville Bishop of daily shows by
a resident band with a special feature
at each performance. The band for
the season was Eddie Hemmings and
his All Star Orchestra with vocalist
Margaret McKechnie in *Swing Along*,
a show advertised as '*The Bandshow
full of Music and Comedy*'. Prior to
his season at Great Yarmouth, Eddie
Hemmings and his orchestra was
the resident band at the Tavistock
Restaurant in London's West End.
Very much in the big band style, the

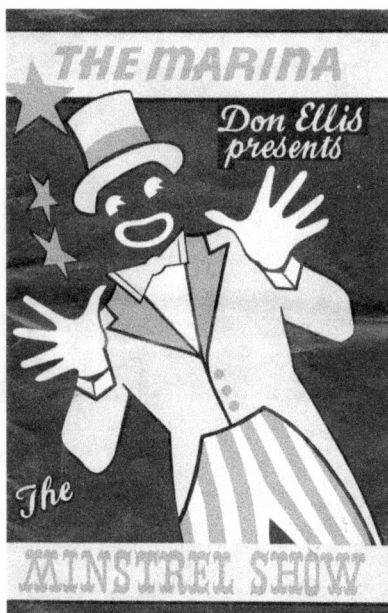

*40. Programme cover for the 1965
Minstrel Show.*

Hemmings orchestra's repertoire ranged from Dixieland and jazz
classics, Latin American dance music and tunes from musical theatre.
Special features ranged from children and adult talent competitions
sponsored by Weston's Biscuits, a *Miss Holiday Girl* Contest for the girl
with the Maltesers Figure sponsored by Mars, a twist competition and
the *Miss Pascall* Bathing Beauty Contest. Yet despite Eddie Hemmings'
best efforts, audience numbers continued to fall away.

In a desperate attempt to revive its flagging fortunes, the Entertainment
and Publicity Committee agreed to the proposal from Don Ellis
Entertainments for a *Minstrel Show* at the Marina from 31 May until
28 August 1965 with the possibility of a week-long extension, drawing
on the current popularity of BBC TV's *Black and White Minstrel Show*.
The *Black and White Minstrel Show* was an extremely popular 45 minute
Saturday night prime time song and dance show featuring the all-male
George Mitchell Minstrel Singers and the all-female BBC Television
Toppers dance troupe, and had viewing figures during 1964 exceeding
21 million per performance. The controversial aspect of the show from a

41. The cast of Don Ellis' Minstrel Show. Singers with blackened faces were not perceived as an issue in 1964. (Archant)

modern perspective was that the all-white Minstrel Singers performed with their faces blackened in the manner of Al Jolson and sang music in a deep-south of America style dressed as Kentucky minstrels. In 1964 it was a popular and acceptable form of entertainment reviving a minstrel tradition that was common in most British holiday resorts during the early 1900s. As well as numerous variety acts linked by the black and white minstrel theme, Don Ellis added the singing star Danny Purches as an extra attraction. Danny Purches, a singer of Romany descent, was discovered by a talent scout while entertaining theatre queues in London's West End. Appearances on the *Six-Five Special* as *'the gypsy with the golden earing'* led to a recording contract and performances in numerous variety shows including a season in Blackpool with the comedian Norman Evans and in *Tom Thumb* at the Alhambra in Bradford. For once the show was a major success. The Great Yarmouth Mercury reported that the *Minstrel Show* was attracting large audiences to the Marina that was *"for many years the White Elephant on Yarmouth's Golden Mile."*[4]

Despite the relative success of the *Minstrel Show*, it was becoming clear to many that the entertainment at the council-run Marina was becoming outdated. Tastes were changing due to the influence of television, especially popular tastes in music. Neither were the financial returns sufficient for the council to afford the top rated stars necessary to compete with those currently appearing at the many alternative venues in the town. Gerry and the Pacemakers and Billy Fury were playing to full houses at the Royal Aquarium while Tommy Steele topped the bill at the Windmill. The outdoor nature of the Marina was also problematic. Audiences were no longer content to pay for a show

THE MARINA

FELIX MANNING

and his

Light

Orchestra

Presents

SUMMER SERENADE

857

42. *Felix Manning and his Orchestra provided holidaymakers with a more gentle musical experience.*

that could be ruined by bad weather. Furthermore, parts of the building were beginning to show signs of wear and were in urgent need of repair. The roof to the covered area was starting to leak. Negotiations by the Entertainment and Publicity Committee to engage the world famous Ivy Benson All Girls Orchestra for the 1966 summer season had also broken down at the last minute. Consequently many members of the town council began questioning whether the Marina as on open-air bandstand had had its day and if the prime site that it occupied on the central promenade could be better served by an alternative facility. In the meantime while the council deliberated over the issue, Felix Manning and his Light Orchestra with singer Clare Ryan were engaged to provide a twice daily music-only show called *Summer Serenade*. Entrance was free but 1/- was charged for the use of a deckchair. Vienna-born violinist Felix Manning was formerly Musical Director of the North Pier Orchestra in Blackpool and prior to his appointment

43. Professor Popcorn and the character Captain Scarlet were a popular attraction for children brought up in the age of television. (Archant)

at the Marina conducted the orchestras at the Talk of the Town and the London Palladium.

For the next few years, while the future of the Marina was in doubt, entertainment took on a more gentle nature. Every morning, Monday to Friday, Professor Popcorn introduced a show for children based on characters from popular television puppet shows including *Thunderbirds*, *Captain Scarlet* and *Joe 90*. In the afternoon it was *Family Fun Time;* 90 minutes of fun, games and comedy from compere Johnny Lee and Jean Lear on the organ. The grand piano was sold as without a resident orchestra it was surplus to requirements. No activities were planned in the evenings except for wrestling competitions on Mondays and Wednesdays. *Listen to the Band* continued to attract on a Sunday. Sections of the covered areas inside and out were let on a short term basis to house shops and static displays. From 1973, a mechanical show under the rear colonnade called *The Magic of Rupert Bear* became a popular feature especially with the children.

Many privately financed schemes were initiated in an effort to attract audiences to the now poorly patronised Marina. In 1970, the *Miss Yarmouth* bathing beauty contest was resurrected by the Town Council and heats held in the Marina every Thursday during the season. In 1973, it was the turn of pop concerts. In May the Publicity and Attractions Committee agreed to the request from the promoter Bruce Benson for the use of the Marina to house weekly pop concerts in June, July and August. Bruce Benson was a young colourful entrepreneur and DJ with many contacts in the music industry and was well-known in popular music circles for his school for DJs at the California Ballroom in Dunstable. Bands engaged to appear included Hot Chocolate, Susie Quatro, Wizard and Medicine Head. The first concert was held on Sunday 10 June and starred Gary Glitter. The official attendance was less than one thousand when between two and three thousand pop fans were expected, although it was clear that many had managed to enter for free. Undeterred, Bruce Benson emphasised that the Glitter concert was a trial run and that audience numbers were expected to increase at subsequent shows. A second concert held on Thursday 21 June, featuring the Sweet, again attracted an audience less than expected. A third concert by Hot Chocolate due to be held on Thursday 28 June was immediately cancelled. In announcing that his committee had decided to abandon all the popular music concerts planned for the Marina, the Director of Publicity and Attractions said that the decision was not due to the small audiences but because of complaints from many residents and businesses in the town about excessive noise, including a strongly worded complaint from the management of the Great Yarmouth General Hospital.

> A series of pop concerts begun at Yarmouth's seafront Marina has been abandoned because of noise. Mr Leslie Shepherd, Director of Publicity and Attractions announcing this yesterday said that there had been complaints of excessive noise following Thursday's concert by the Sweet. [5]

44. Danny Arnold's Cowtown USA, a popular attraction for the young. (YPD/YL)

All efforts to improve the standing of the Marina having failed, the Town Council reluctantly decided that the best course of action was to replace the dated Marina by a more modern up-to-date facility. Consequently, at a meeting of the Publicity and Amenities Committee that was held on 15 October 1974, it was decided to offer a limited lease for the use of the building in an attempt to revive its flagging fortunes until such a time as the site was ready to be redeveloped. Various proposals were received for possible short term functions for the Marina including developing the interior for use as a dinosaur park, a lion cub nursery for Chipperfield's circus or as a Wild West museum. The committee eventually agreed to accept a proposal from Mr Danny Arnold of Margate for a 4 year lease at a rent of £9500 per annum to convert the inside of the building into a Wild West complex. The complex was planned to include an open area for entertainments, a museum, shops, a saloon and a jail. Work on the conversion was completed in time for a grand opening on the 1 June 1975, including the conversion of the outside to give the appearance of a Wild West township and the addition of an artificial mountain range on the top deck.

45. The Wild West comes to Yarmouth. Visitors could have their photographs inserted onto Wanted posters in the mock jail. (YPD/YL)

'Sheriff' Danny Arnold was no novice in Wild West re-enactments. For the previous 14 years, the alleged ex-Texas sheriff had staged Wild West tableaux in the Golden Garter Saloon at the Cliftonville Lido in Margate. Consequently, from its opening Danny Arnold's *Cowtown USA* at the Marina became a popular attraction especially with the young. Static exhibits included a museum of Indian and Wild West artefacts, a souvenir shop, a replica jail and the Golden Horseshoe Saloon. In the shop visitors were encouraged to buy postcards embossed with a Wells Fargo Pony Express seal, badges displaying photographs of Sheriff Danny Arnold and pictorial maps of the Wild West showing the various pioneer trails and places where incidents of importance took place. In the jail, visitors could have their photographs inserted onto 'Wanted' posters. Regular displays of horsemanship and other cowboy associated skills took place in the open central area. Each display was preceded by the appearance on the promenade of a cowboy on horseback. Horseshoes painted on the pavement showed the way to the entrance. Cowboy songs accompanied displays of lassoing and whip cracking. Willing volunteers bravely held on to sheets of newspaper while an expert cowboy cut them into pieces with a whip. Each display finished with an extremely theatrical Wild West shoot out in which Sheriff Danny Arnold was the only one left alive by the end of the action.

A reporter from the Yarmouth Mercury commented that *Cowtown USA* had transformed the Marina from a white elephant on the promenade and regular loss maker to something that was of considerable benefit to local ratepayers.[6] Not for the first time was that description applied to the Marina and not for the first time was the hope expressed of a revival in the fortunes of the venue. Unfortunately, not everyone was as enthusiastic. At a meeting of the Publicity and Amenities Committee, Councillor Miller said that the attraction was simply hideous and Councillor Bunwell called it a monstrosity in the centre of the seafront. An attempt to move the attraction to a less central position at the Nelson Gardens failed. Councillor Miller suggested that the Pleasure Beach was the right location for Cowtown. *"I don't care where it goes as long as it gets out of the way,"*[7] he added. *Cowtown USA* continued to attract visitors until the end of the 1978 summer season when all activities at the Marina ceased and the building was cleared prior to demolition.

---

1   NRO YTC 88/47, p73, 14 October 1959.
2   NRO YTC 88/48 1960-61, E&PC p283, 9 November 1960.
3   NRO YTC 88/48 1960-61, E&PC p173, 7 September 1960.
4   Yarmouth Mercury, 2 September 1965.
5   Eastern Evening News, 28 June 1973.
6   *Ibid. 4*, 12 September 1975.
7   Eastern Daily Press, 3 March 1976.

8

The Final Curtain

For some members of Great Yarmouth's Town Council and for many residents of the town, the 1937 Marina project was not only ill-conceived and backward-looking but also a golden opportunity missed. An unroofed and unheated music enclosure in a prime position on the resort's main promenade, in which most of the audience sat on canvas chairs unprotected from the unreliable weather, was not considered by many to be the best of investments, especially as its use was restricted solely to the warmer summer months. The hope expressed at the opening ceremony on 1 July 1937 by Mr. Ellis, Chairman of the Beach and Promenade Committee, that the Marina would not only provide holidaymakers with a location for musical entertainment but also act as a conference centre was optimistic at best. It was considered by many people to be an unsuitable design for hosting conferences and the difficulties experienced by the Municipal Orchestra showed it not to be sufficiently adaptable to cope with all forms of musical entertainment. A roofed enclosure with the same capacity would not only have provided an all year round building suitable for all kinds of music, but also a general facility for conferences and other communal activities unavailable elsewhere in the region and of immense potential benefit to the economy of the town.

Yet the Marina concept was consistent with the prevailing views of the time regarding the nature of a seaside holiday and the needs of a premier resort. For the first twenty years of its forty-two year existence, the Marina was a well-loved and well-used summertime attraction and might have proved an even more profitable facility for the Town Council had it not been for the five years of enforced inactivity due to World War Two. Unfortunately by the early 1960s, circumstances, tastes and expectations had changed to such an extent that the unroofed Marina could not be adapted to accommodate them. Factory workers from the industrial midlands no longer came to Great Yarmouth just for the health-giving benefits of the bracing sea air. The fashion of the day was to laze in the sun and most visitors to the resort preferred their entertainment to be under cover and in the dry rather than outside where they were often prone to being buffeted by wind and rain. Tastes in music had also changed. Loud rock 'n' roll was a popular choice, especially with the young, and the resulting noise pollution was often an issue with an open-topped auditorium close to a residential area. Where modern amplified music was concerned the Marina could not compete with the conventional enclosed theatres at the Windmill, Royal Aquarium and Britannia Pier.

The benefits that could have been provided by a roofed enclosure were soon patently obvious, especially after the loss-making season of 1946. In May 1947, Councillor A.W. Chittleburgh, the incumbent chairman of the Entertainments and Publicity Committee, initiated the first of many inquiries looking into the possibility of providing a roof over the Marina and improving the versatility of the facility. He suggested that with a roof the Marina would become a suitable location for a Rollerdrome, boxing arena and conference hall as well as a facility for concerts and dances. He even suggested that it could be converted into a Lido. The main stumbling block at the time was a lack of financial resources as well as a national shortage of building materials. Also there was little incentive in the 1950s for the Council to embark on an expensive project that they could barely afford when, at that time during the best days of the British seaside holiday industry, the Marina was showing a financial profit. However, in 1962, as competition from Continental package holidays increased, the Town Council became aware that the improvements being made to the Empire Stadium at

Wembley involved the construction of an encircling roof of aluminium and glass over the whole of the seating area. At the 1962 November meeting of the Entertainments and Publicity Committee, it was agreed to commission a report from the contractors at Wembley regarding the possibility of constructing a similar roof over the auditorium of the Marina.[1] When the report was received from the contractors, it clearly indicated that roofing the Marina would require serious and expensive structural modifications to the building itself. A roof similar to that at Wembley could be installed for £20,000 but as Councillor Edgar Barker commented *"that expense would result in just a big old structure with a roof on. It would certainly not be an indoor theatre."*[2] Two or three times that expense would be required to bring the Marina up to the standard necessary for it to function as an indoor theatre and he could see no real demand for a 3000 seater conference centre in Great Yarmouth. It was, therefore, decided that the council would take no further action on this matter now or in the future due to the potentially high and unaffordable costs likely to be incurred.[3] It was reluctantly agreed that roofing the Marina by the Town Council was no longer a viable possibility.

Despite its apparent unsuitability for conferences, the Marina was used as the venue for many summertime rallies. From 1950 until 1962, the Norfolk Old Folks Clubs' Rally was held at the Marina, initially in the second week of June and then during Pensioners' Week in September, with entertainment provided by the resident band. That the rallies held in 1952 and 1953 were rain affected did not deter the organisers from using the venue again.

The old people mingled with the holiday audience and gave

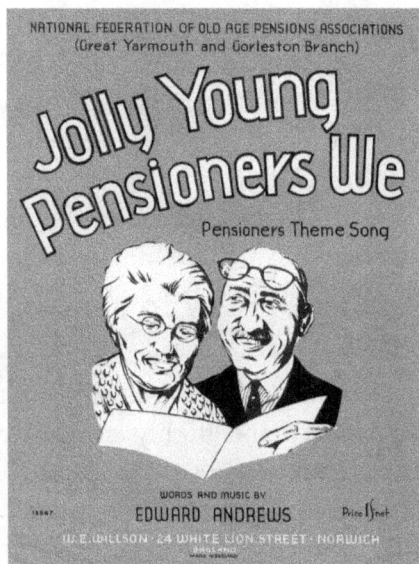

46. *Jolly Young Pensioners We; not even bad weather could dampen their spirits.*

every indication of thoroughly enjoying themselves when the band burlesqued the old-time music hall during the first half of the performance they joined with great gusto in the singing of the songs of yesteryear including *Honeysuckle and the Bee* and *Who were you with Last Night?*.[4]

The annual parade through Great Yarmouth on Commonwealth Youth Sunday by contingents from the sea cadets, boy's brigade, scouts, guides, cubs, ATC cadets, Red Cross cadets, Girl's Life Brigade, St John's cadets and the band of the Salvation Army always ended with a service and gathering at the Marina. Other annual rallies were held on behalf of the National Union of Agricultural Workers, the British Legion and the East Anglian Brass Band Association. On 4 July 1968, American Independence Day, a festival was held at the Marina to celebrate the developing links between the USA and Great Yarmouth due to the discovery and exploitation of North Sea gas and oil.

British holidaymakers and American oil families joined yesterday evening in an American Independence Day commemoration at the Marina...... The festival included a tribute in music to America played by the Yarmouth Salvation Army Citadel Band under Bandmaster Robert Cox. ... It was preceded by a parade to the Marina which included the Salvation Army Band, the USAF colour party from Lakenheath under Staff Sgt. James Sartain, and American children carrying placards bearing the names of their home states.[5]

By 1968, it was clear that the Marina and the entertainment it provided was not only becoming dated and old fashioned in the context of a modern and highly competitive holiday industry. It was equally clear that it was also non-profitable and starting to become a drain on the council's financial resources. Heated discussions ensued as the Entertainments and Publicity Committee was forced to consider a future policy for the Marina and the nature of the council's involvement in its running. Various ideas were mooted, including continuing the current use of the building with the same kind of entertainment, retaining the building solely as a sitting out area, or demolishing the building and replacing it with a car park and toilets. A suggestion that it should become an annexe of the Maritime Museum for East Anglia and a suitable site for preserving and exhibiting the wherry Olga was quickly rejected. The preferred solution was for the redevelopment of the whole central site including the Marina, the existing small car park and the open-air swimming pool. At a meeting on 12 July 1968 the committee resolved to invite offers from all interested parties for leasing either the interior of the Marina or the whole central site on a short or long term basis, and their ideas for its development and use. The sole requirement was that any suggested scheme should necessarily include the provision of public toilet facilities.

Proposals were eventually received from Botton Brothers Ltd, Jays Entertainments and Dale Martin Promotions. Albert and Jim Botton were originally from a fairground background and had been managing the Pleasure Beach in Great Yarmouth since 1942. Jays Entertainments was another Great Yarmouth-based family firm, the owners in 1968 of the Windmill Theatre, the Empire Cinema and other properties and clubs in the town including the Penrice Arms, home of the Great Yarmouth Jazz Club. The Hippodrome Circus was added to their assets in 1979. Dale Martin Promotions was a London-based firm with sporting interests and had already been heavily involved in organising wrestling competitions at the Marina. Presentations of all three proposals for the future of the Marina site were given to a meeting of the Seafront Committee on 20 March 1970. After some discussion, on 24 March the Seafront Committee agreed in principle to accept the proposal from the Botton Brothers and requested them to submit a more detailed development plan.

The scheme that was submitted to the Seafront Committee on 26 July 1971 on behalf of the Botton Brothers required the demolition of the existing Marina building, replacing it by a new construction with a transparent roof housing a Dolphin Pool with tiered seating, 12 shops, a stage area, a licensed restaurant, public bar and new public toilets; the whole to be on a 21 year lease from the council with the option of a further 21 years. Possession of the site was required from October 1971. After due deliberation, the proposal was rejected by the Council as it constituted a substantial departure from the ideas presented at the meeting in the previous March. As well as inviting the Botton Brothers to resubmit revised plans, the Seafront Committee stated that they would also consider new proposals from other interested parties.

As a result, an ambitious proposal to lease the Marina site for a period of 42 years was received from Channel Island Securities Ltd, a Jersey-based developer, and, after some discussion, was accepted in principle at a meeting of the Seafront Committee on 17 February 1972. After completing a geological survey of the site, Channel Island Securities presented a more detailed plan to the Seafront Committee on 12 July 1972 for replacing the Marina by a large two storied building; the ground floor to be operational by the summer of 1973 and the upper floor by 1974. The ground floor was designed to house a wide range of activities operated by individual concessionaires under the management of a new Marina Company. These were to include a restaurant, six shops, a bar, a bingo hall, an amusement arcade and new public toilets. The upper floor, scheduled to be completed a year later, was planned to include a £200,000 auditorium with stage to give facilities for wrestling, shows and other entertainment, a sunbathing roof garden, a night club and a child's play area. Unfortunately, negotiations ran into difficulties and the proposal was eventually withdrawn. A new proposal received from J. Larter and K. Sparkes of the Larter Group was again approved in principle but again withdrawn after the council and the developer failed to agree on its details. The entrepreneur and developer, Joe Larter, was born in Martham and in 1983 founded the successful Pleasurewood Hills adventure centre near to Lowestoft. With little progress being made regarding a long term solution for the Marina, in October 1974 the committee agreed the aforementioned four year lease with Danny Arnold for the existing building to be used as a Wild West complex.[6]

A second revised development plan was submitted by the Botton Brothers to the Seafront Committee in April 1975 proposing a rebuild of the Marina to include a central covered auditorium, peripheral shops, public bars and amusements, which was again approved in principle. The cost of the redevelopment was estimated at £300,000. A lease of 21 years was agreed at an initial rent of £4000 per annum. Once again, the agreement between the two parties was jinxed as the Botton Brothers were forced to withdraw on the death of the senior partner Albert Botton, after which the firm was transferred to his son-in-law, Jimmy Jones.[7] In the aftermath of their sudden withdrawal, further proposals were received from Danny Arnold, Peter Jay on behalf of Jays Entertainments and Willow Spring Ltd. Under Danny Arnold's proposal, the existing Marina would be demolished and replaced with a Wild West City, motion picture house, shops, bars and a restaurant. Both the Willow Spring's and Peter Jay's proposals involved converting the main portion of the site into a Continental style open-air market. The proposal that gained the greatest approval among the members of the Seafront Committee was received from the Norwich-based East Anglian Securities Ltd and its subsidiary Forsanet Properties in which the existing Marina was to be replaced by a large rectangular building designed to house a synthetic skating ring for summer use and an indoor bowls rink for the winter, as well as restaurants, catering and entertainment facilities.

By the early 1970s, some members of the Town Council were concerned that the proposals they had received for the development of the Marina site mostly replicated facilities already available on the promenade and were exclusively aimed at the holiday trade. Few of the suggested amenities would be of much benefit to the ordinary residents of the town or add to the economy of the area outside of the holiday season. The Director of the Seafront Committee also went so far as to suggest that the members of the Town Council should consider submitting a scheme of their own and, following discussions with the Borough Treasurer, indicated how such a scheme could be financed from a Capital Expenditure Programme. All that was needed was an innovative project that would not only be an attraction during the holiday season but would also be of all year round benefit for the residents of the town. A visit by Councillor Leslie Shepherd to the Isle of Man following the disastrous fire at the Summerland Pleasure-Dome in 1973, gave rise to the idea of a leisure centre. While the fire was a disaster, the concept of an all-year-round leisure complex on the seafront at Great Yarmouth appealed to many members of the Town Council.

47. Demolition 1979. An ignominious end to a much-loved seaside facility. (NCC/PN)

In 1976, the national focus was definitely on leisure and Great Yarmouth's contribution was as the host to a Festival of Sport. When opening the festival, the Mayor, Mr Alex Laird, indicated that the newly-formed Great Yarmouth Borough Council was seeking a site for a sports centre in the town. Promoted initially by the Labour government of Harold Wilson, the great expansion in public amenities during the 1960s and '70s was in sports and leisure centres, purpose built and freely available to all. By the 1960s, most people had more money in their pockets which, combined with a shorter working week, enabled them to spend more time on leisure activities. Sport was being promoted as a means for developing a positive community focus as well as for its obvious health benefits, especially in the twenty-seven post-war new towns. In order to encourage year-round participation, especially by women, sporting opportunities were needed that were under cover. The absence of indoor facilities was inhibiting participation in sport by a large portion of the population. Television had also introduced the viewing public to a wider range of sporting activities beyond just the Saturday afternoon men's football and cricket. The first sports centre was completed in 1964 at Harlow in Essex. By the mid-1970s, sports and leisure centres had become the fashion.

Finding the ideal location for a sports centre in Great Yarmouth was not easy. Neither the Wellesley nor the Beaconsfield sports grounds was considered large enough to accommodate a building of any size. With the outdated outside swimming pool also needing replacement, it did not take much prompting from the Mayor and the Great Yarmouth Sports Council for the Marina site to become recognised as the most likely location for a combined indoor sports centre and swimming pool. Following tentative enquiries with other leisure centres and a feasibility study by the Treasurer, on 2 November 1977 the Publicity and Amenities Committee accepted a proposal from a sub-committee consisting of Councillors Stone, Miller (the current Mayor), Scott and Stone for the Council to consider the development of a combined Sports and Leisure Pool Complex on the site of the Marina.

To help in the planning, members of both the Great Yarmouth Sports Council and the Borough Council made a fact finding visit to the newly-opened Leisure Pool in Rotherham on Friday 10 March 1978. The Rotherham Leisure Pool Complex opened in 1974 and was unique in that its innovative pool design broke away from the conventional rectangular pool, replacing it with smaller fun pools, a beach and a main pool equipped with a wave machine. Following this visit, at a joint meeting of the Policy & Resources, Finance and Publicity & Amenities Committees it was agreed to develop the whole central promenade site as a combined Leisure Centre and Pool Complex. Module 2 was appointed to design the building and to supervise its construction, East Cheap Investments of Manchester were given responsibility for organising the project's finance and the management of the finished complex was entrusted to Trust House Forte. While the building was to remain wholly in the Council's ownership, net profits were allocated 50% to the council and 25% each to East Cheap Investments and Trust House Forte. The final go-ahead was given at a full council meeting on 3 October 1978 with the project financed by a lease back arrangement with the Pension Fund subject to the approval of its trustees.

The closed Marina, once described as the star attraction on the east coast, suffered an ignominious end. The empty building fell victim to inexplicable wanton vandalism. Peggotty, in his column in the Eastern Evening News lamented that:

> The Council did remove expensive coin-operated lavatory door locks and other items of value that could be used... Anything left behind has been smashed to pieces. Three quarters of the perimeter of the circular building was glazed – and, of course, the intruders made short work of the panes. Not one of the hundreds remains. In fact in most cases the glass has been completely broken out, not simply holed in the middle, and you walk on a lethal carpet. That must have been a noisy exercise by the vandals, shattering glass, but they succeeded without being heard. Anything capable of being ripped up, pulled down, hauled off, jumped on or kicked in has been ripped up, pulled down, etc.[8]

Work on replacing the Marina with the new leisure centre began at the end of January 1979 and was completed in time for it to be opened on Monday 14 June 1981 by sportsman Duncan Goodhew.

> Yarmouth's impressive new Marina Centre opened with a grand splash yesterday. Before an invited audience of local dignitaries and pressmen from all over the country, Olympic swimming star Duncan Goodhew unveiled a plaque to mark the climax of three years planning and building.[9]

In his speech, the Mayor, Mr Gordon Chapman, inadvertently echoed some of the sentiments uttered at the opening of the old Marina in 1937.

> The prospects for the youth of our borough for 12 months of the year are tremendous ... The covered recreation area would become the envy of the other seaside towns throughout the country. This project will encourage the reputation of Great Yarmouth as Britain's number one holiday resort.[10]

The completed new Marina complex was equipped with a sports hall, 4 squash courts, a fitness room and multi-gym, a restaurant, piazza,

48. The newly opened Marina Leisure Centre, bringing an outdoor seaside feeling to an indoor swimming-pool. (Archant)

children's play area and leisure pool designed as an outdoor beach environment with a warm Mediterranean atmosphere, a wave machine and the inevitable but necessary public toilets.

Peggotty again provided a fitting epitaph for the old Marina in his column by commenting that:

> Although in the past decade or so the Marina open-air amphitheatre on Yarmouth's Golden Mile has been a white elephant, during its 40 years' life it gave pleasure to many people – chiefly holidaymakers, naturally.[11]

1   NRO Y/TC EPC 14 November 1962.
2   Eastern Daily Press, 11 November 1962.
3   NRO Y/TC EPC 9 January 1962, p353.
4   Yarmouth Mercury, 9 September 1955.
5   Eastern Evening News, 5 July 1968.
6   See Chapter 7.
7   NRO YTC 88/63
8   *Ibid. 5*, 20 January 1979.
9   Eastern Daily Press, Tuesday 15 June 1981.
10   *Ibid.*
11   *Ibid. 5*, 20 January 1979.

Index

www.ingramcontent.com/pod-product-compliance
Lightning Source LLC
LaVergne TN
LVHW021133080426
835509LV00010B/1343